ARCO

Literary Critiques

Tennyson

J. B. Steane

New York

To Margaret Pendle

Acknowledgements

The cover picture of Tennyson and the photograph by Julia Margaret Cameron are reproduced by kind permission of the *Radio Times* Hulton Picture Library; the portrait of George Clayton Tennyson the younger by permission of Macmillan & Co. Ltd.; Samuel Laurence's portrait of the poet by permission of the Trustees of the National Portrait Gallery; the sketch by J. Spedding by permission of the Mansell Collection; and the Beerbohm caricature by permission of William Heinemann Ltd.

Published 1969 by ARCO PUBLISHING COMPANY, INC.
219 Park Avenue South, New York, N.Y. 10003
Copyright © J. B. Steane, 1966, 1969
All Rights Reserved
Library of Congress Catalog Number 75-78854
Printed in the United States of America

Arco Literary Critiques

Of recent years, the ordinary man who reads for pleasure has been gradually excluded from that great debate in which every intelligent reader of the classics takes part. There are two reasons for this: first, so much criticism floods from the world's presses that no one but a scholar living entirely among books can hope to read it all; and second, the critics and analysts, mostly academics, use a language that only their fellows in the same discipline can understand.

Consequently criticism, which should be as 'inevitable as breathing'—an activity for which we are all qualified—has become the private field of a few warring factions who shout their unintelligible battle cries to each other but make little communication to the common man.

Arco Literary Critiques aims at giving a straightforward account of literature and of writers—straightforward both in content and in language. Critical jargon is as far as possible avoided; any terms that must be used are explained simply; and the constant preoccupation of the authors of the Series is to be lucid.

It is our hope that each book will be easily understood, that it will adequately describe its subject without pretentiousness so that the intelligent reader who wants to know about Donne or Keats or Shakespeare will find enough in it to bring him up to date on critical estimates.

Even those who are well read, we believe, can benefit from a lucid exposition of what they may have taken for granted, and perhaps—dare it be said?—not fully understood.

K. H. G.

Tennyson

'Tennyson' is still an emotionally-toned word. One can say 'I'm doing Spenser' (or Chaucer or Browning or Pope or Words-worth) and nobody is likely to react with surprise, derision, gratification or any particularly lively emotion at all. But the name of Tennyson still provokes a wry smile, an ironical lift of the eyebrows, or their stern depression into the frown that signifies critical disapproval and dismissal. Favourable reactions çan be equally emphatic. A toast to Tennyson is often coupled mentally with a proposition like 'Fair play for the Victorians', and behind it may well lie the notion that, as the Victorian age was generally derided in the first half of this century, it is safe to assume that tastes will have in the second changed and that the Victorians are now 'in'.

So I think that one's first effort in reading Tennyson (of all poets) must be to clear the mind of associations and attitudes formed there by habit rather than judgement, or by fashion rather than taste. Just how difficult this may be I realise only too well, having tried to accomplish it in this book. I have no great conviction of success; some hope, however, that it may help a few long-familiar poems to be read afresh, serving also to introduce others, and to place them against the background of a life and a century. Above all, I would like it to help confirm that though Tennyson has many limitations, he is an *abiding* poet. He himself ruefully spoke of a day when—

> I shall be forgotten by old Time,
> Laid on the shelf.

At least that day has not come yet.

J. B. S.

4

Contents

1. Somersby: The Tennyson Family   *page* 9

2. Earliest Poems: 'The Devil and the Lady'   16

3. Cambridge   26

4. Poems: 1830, 1832 and 1842   34

5. Hallam's Death: Tennyson's Marriage   59

6. 'In Memoriam'   72

7. 'Maud' and Farringford   88

8. 'Idylls of the King'   113

9. Old Age and Aldworth   128

10. Conclusion   144

    Bibliography   156

    General Index   158

    Index to Tennyson's Works   160

Alfred Tennyson by Samuel Laurence (c. 1840)

Photograph of Tennyson taken in 1865 by Julia Margaret Cameron

'Mr. Tennyson reading *In Memoriam* to his sovereign', from *The Poets' Corner* by Max Beerbohm

I

Somersby: The Tennyson Family

'They are all strangely brought up' (Tennyson's grandfather)

'The son of a clergyman in affluent circumstances, life from the first was made smooth and pleasant for him.' So said *The Times* in its obituary columns on October 7, 1892, and so indeed it seemed. The Poet Laureate had passed away peacefully in a moonlit room near Haslemere; he had lived in the relaxing sunshine and shade of Farringford and Aldworth, emerging from time to time to read *In Memoriam* to his sovereign; and eighty-three years earlier he had been born in a Lincolnshire village called Somersby where life must surely have been as delightful as the agreeable name seemed to promise.

So much was common knowledge, or at least general belief. The Rectory would be set, as in the poet's *Ode to Memory*, amidst orchard and garden with 'sweet forget-me-nots', and with the famous brook which loved—

> To purl o'er matted cress and ribbed sand,
> Or dimple in the dark of rushy coves.

The summer would bring family visits to the seaside at Mablethorpe, another kindly name. Then there must have been a houseful of children (twelve of them), a gentle mother—

> The stately flower of female fortitude,
> Of perfect wifehood and pure lowlihead

ISABEL

—and the father, Doctor Tennyson himself, no ordinary country parson, but a scholar, and a descendant, it was claimed, of the

9

d'Eyncourts and the Plantagenets. No wonder *The Times* could feel that fortune had smiled on the poet at his birth and been fairly consistent in its favours ever since.

Sad to tell, the truth was darker and harder. Tennyson's childhood certainly had its blessings, but there were times when he wished he were dead. At the root of the family distresses was an injustice done to Dr. Tennyson by his own father, who disliked him and refused to treat him to the privileges of the eldest son. Perhaps there was reason for this. Grandfather Tennyson had made money, turning from law to business, sharpening a keen eye for profit (the fishing industry at Grimsby was prospering and new docks were needed), marrying profitably too, and then pushing his way, as *nouveau riche*, into the ranks of the gentry, with a seat in Parliament for himself and an enviable inheritance for his favourite son. The poet's father did not qualify for that position, however, and it was Charles, the younger son, who benefited. No doubt old Tennyson had his reasons. Certainly the later development of the two brothers suggests that, from his own point of view, he made the right decision. Charles, correct, ambitious and hard-working, was a thoroughly conventional credit to the family; George (Alfred's father) was not. On the other hand, there is also no doubt that, however much George's 'black-bloodedness' was native to him, it was further embittered and poisoned by the sense that his life had been cramped within intolerable bounds by the very hand that normally would have enriched it. An acquaintance of old Tennyson's told him plainly over the dinner-table that his treatment of the elder son was against nature: 'Tennyson, if you do this you'll certainly be damned, you will indeed'. Undeterred, he sent George to an obscure private tutor, and Charles to Eton; and it was Charles who inherited the estate of Bayons Manor, while George had to make do with the Rectory of Somersby and Bag Enderby.

Holy Orders were therefore the lot of a man whose temperament seems to have been as little suited to them as was his appearance. His portrait (facing page 65) might be that of an actor, a gipsy, an artist; a man, one would think, of strong passions, perhaps a heavy drinker, perhaps violent; or, taking a long shot, it might be an artist's imaginary impression of Emily Brontë's Heathcliffe, and one would never feel easy in the presence of its original. At any rate, one would not suppose him to be the Rector of Somersby and Bag Enderby. He was six-foot two, athletic, strong-boned and swarthy. Like his son Alfred he had a magnificent speaking voice and there was something alien and unEnglish about his appearance. His children took after him. 'All but Frederick,' we read, 'were of a gipsy darkness and the girls were as handsome as the boys' (when Alfred went abroad he rarely found himself placed as an Englishman, and in Ireland he was once thought to be a French spy preparing for the invasion of Erin). Mrs. Tennyson no doubt contributed her share to the striking appearance of the family, for she was a great beauty and had had as many as twenty-five proposals of marriage. Some of the Lincolnshire parishioners must have felt that the folk at the Rectory had an ungodly allowance of good looks.

Certainly there were happiness and goodness in the family to match. Both parents were intelligent people with lively interests, and Dr. Tennyson was a genuine scholar. The children's games often took a literary turn: stories would be written, put under the vegetable dishes at dinner, and then read aloud when the meal was over. The poet's son Hallam, in his two-volume *Memoir* written shortly after Tennyson's death, gives a pleasant description of the children's evening entertainments:

> In the winter evenings by the firelight little Alfred would take her [Cecilia, Hallam's aunt who had described the scene to him] on his knee, with Arthur and Matilda leaning against him on either side, the baby Horatio between his legs; and how he would fascinate this group of young hero-worshippers who listened open-eared and open-mouthed to legends of knights and heroes among untravelled forests rescuing distressed damsels, or to his tales about Indians, or demons or witches. The brothers and sisters would sometimes act one of the old English plays; and the elder members of the family thought that my father, from his dramatic rendering of the parts and his musical voice, would turn out to be an actor.

This is well enough: the scene is a little bit 'arranged', like a Victorian painting, but no doubt the truth was something like that. And no doubt there was much more in childhood which blessed the whole family and which Alfred would later recollect with affection.

School was not amongst these things. He was sent to Louth School in 1815 and it remained a dreaded memory for ever after. 'How I did hate that school!' When the Headmaster caned him he was unable to hold his knife and fork for several days, and he remembered one poor creature 'who was so brutally flogged for not knowing his lesson that he had to stay in bed for six weeks'. After this it was a great relief to come home (for he was withdrawn in 1820) and have lessons with father, though the principal item in his education seems to have been a hard daily grind at Horace, whom Tennyson came to hate. When in old age he complained, 'They use *me* as lesson-books at school, and they will call me "that horrible Tennyson" ', it was the thought of becoming a latter-day Horace to new generations of school-boys that most distressed him. But it was not Dr. Tennyson's teaching that upset Alfred; rather the terrible fits of anger and despair that would come upon him. These were extreme enough to drive the boy out of the house at night to fling himself down in the churchyard and pray for death as a release from the pain of seeing his parents in such affliction.

As time went on Dr. Tennyson's 'black blood' thickened. It is hard, in fact, not to see life at Somersby Rectory as a sort of cross between *Wuthering Heights* and *The Way of all Flesh*. The servants snarl and rage in the background. There was Horlins the coachman, 'half mad and generally half drunk'. He one day came roaring into the drawing room, threw the harness down on the floor, and shouted, 'Clean it thyself, then'. There was the cook, also touchy when criticised, summing up the Rector and his wife with a fine turn of phrase: 'If you raked out Hell with a small toothcomb, you wouldn't find their likes'. This cook was eventually burnt to death and Dr. Tennyson injured himself badly while trying to save her. Even that went against him, for as Sir Charles Tennyson (the poet's grandson) puts it:

'the story soon became current in Lincolnshire that he had given orders for a butt of water to be kept in future by the kitchen door, so that any cook who caught fire could jump into it, and extinguish herself without troubling her master'. Then there was a Calvinist aunt, who occasionally paid a visit to impress the youngsters with a dire sense of things to come. 'Alfred, Alfred', she used to say, 'when I look at you I think of the words of Holy Scripture—"Depart from me, ye cursed, into everlasting fire" '. This might be shrugged off, but not the bitter recriminations which circulated in the various branches of the Tennyson family, nor the deterioration of Dr. Tennyson's health, leading him to increased bouts of violence and to drink. Some phrases from a painful letter which the doctor wrote to his father in 1820 make the bitterness of his spirits all too clear. He refers to 'the rude and unprecedented manner in which you first addressed me at Hainton, after a long absence, on your return from York (I quote your own words, "Now, you great awkward booby, are you here?")'. He also complains of 'the unprovoked and sarcastic remarks . . . which in your last visit were levelled against the father of a large family in the very presence of his children and that father between forty and fifty years of age'. As the children grew up, so the father seems to have lost all real control over himself. His mental aberrations sometimes wore a comical aspect, as when he had to turn away from the house of a person he was about to visit because he could not remember his own name (he then met a friend who said 'Hello, Tennyson', and, thus enlightened, felt able to return to the house he had just left). But generally there was little enough to laugh at. To his wife he began to use 'degrading language' and with the increase of his drunkenness she eventually felt that she could not continue to live with him. His violence took an uglier turn still. He carried a loaded gun and tried to fire it through the kitchen window. He also carried a knife and with it threatened to kill his eldest son Frederick. This was the state of affairs at home during the time when Alfred was at Cambridge. Occasionally, amidst general thanksgiving, Dr. Tennyson would take himself off to Paris to stay with a family friend. But there was little peace until 1831, when at the age of fifty-two he died. He had been a remarkable, gifted, unlucky man, and Alfred mourned his death sincerely. The next week he slept in the dead man's bed and earnestly desired (so he told his own son) to see his father's ghost. But the perturbed spirit was evidently at rest.

Plenty of troubles remained with the family. Alfred himself was not exactly the strongest, solidest pillar of normality, yet on him much of the father's responsibility devolved. Mrs. Tennyson wept a great deal: 'Dam your eyes, mother, dam your eyes', the poet used to say to her in later years, affectionately and half-humorously, though Sir Harold Nicolson's version adds a letter to the verb and a new flavour to the remark. His sister Emily, who became engaged to Tennyson's great friend Arthur Hallam, suffered a breakdown when Hallam died suddenly in 1833. For Alfred, Hallam's death was the greatest single sorrow of his life, but he still remained the chief support his mother and sisters had. Frederick, the eldest of the brothers, was a brilliant, unmanageable and unhelpful creature, who had no doubt hastened his father's end by being rusticated from Cambridge for three terms and running up enormous debts in the rest of his time there. He was described as 'sinister in aspect and terrific in manner, even to the discomfiture of elderly dons'. In 1834 he left Somersby for Italy to enjoy sunshine and music: he was the most fortunate of Alfred's brothers. Of the others, Charles, miserable with neuralgia, went into the Church and for a time took to opium, 'making no use of either body or soul', as Frederick said; Septimus languished in a solicitor's office, then became broody and listless (Sir Charles Tennyson tells Rossetti's story of a visitor to the Hallams' House in Wimpole Street 'who, on being shown into the drawing-room, was amazed to see a large, swarthy man arise from the hearth-rug where he had been lying at full length, and advance with outstretched hand, saying in a deep voice: "I am Septimus, the most morbid of the Tennysons" '); and Edward, the most tragic of them, lost his reason. Tennyson described his condition: 'He weeps bitterly sometimes and says that his mind is so wretched that he is scarcely able to endure his existence'. He lived on, however, confined to a mental home and enduring it for nearly sixty years.

Such was the family in which Alfred's strongly emotional, affectionate and anxious nature was so largely bound up. They were all very close, thrown much into each other's company, taking their recreations together, even for much of the time sleeping five or six in a room. The pain of seeing so many he loved suffer so grievously is hard to exaggerate. Tennyson is sometimes described as the most melancholy of our poets: considering his circumstances, I think he is probably among the strongest and most resilient.

In 1831 two of the children, Mary and Arthur, visited grandfather Tennyson at Bayons Manor. The old man who was himself so largely responsible for what had gone awry considered his grandchildren with dismay and perplexity: 'I don't know what Arthur is fit for . . . He must be instructed before he can be fit for anything. His gestures and twitchings etc. are ridiculous and he would be a subject for ridicule anywhere'. And, as he turned over the whole deplorable situation: 'They are all strangely brought up'.

George Clayton Tennyson the younger, the poet's father

2

Earliest Poems: 'The Devil and the Lady'

'It is wonderful how the whelp could have
known such things' (Dr. Jowett)

Poetry played an important part in the strange upbringing. The
children read it, and most of them wrote it, as naturally as they
learned to talk. Alfred was best. He could hardly remember a time
when poetry was not a part of his life. As an old man he recalled
that at the age of eight he covered both sides of his blackboard
with lines in praise of flowers, written in blank verse in the style
of James Thomson, author of *The Seasons* and the only poet
Tennyson knew at this time. 'About ten or eleven', he goes on,
'Pope's *Homer's Iliad* became a favourite of mine and I wrote
hundreds of lines in the regular Popeian metre, nay even could
improvise them; so could my two elder brothers, for my father
was a poet and could write regular metre very skilfully.' At
about twelve he was writing a six-thousand-line epic in the style
of Sir Walter Scott, and at fourteen his hero was Byron. 'A day
when the whole world seemed to be darkened for me', he said
of 19 April, 1824; and on a rock at Holywell he carved the words
'Byron is dead'. But it was about this time that his brother
Frederick whispered to him: 'I've got a poet who is much finer
than Byron', and thus they discovered Shelley, who for another
hundred years was still to be the poet of youth. His infectious
enthusiasm and the heady music of his verse were potent among
young readers till fairly recent times; but no one in their teens
seems to 'see Shelley plain' nowadays, and thereon no doubt
hangs a whole cultural history if one cared to follow it up. In
published criticism of his earlier work, reviewers often coupled

16

Tennyson's name with Shelley's. The modern critic and poet William Empson talks of Romanticism as 'a sense of hugging to oneself a private dream-world' and there is much of this in both poets. Somewhat Shelleyan too is this famous reminiscence of Tennyson's: 'Before I could read I was in the habit on a stormy day of spreading my arms to the wind, and crying out "I hear a voice that's speaking in the wind", and the words "far, far away" had always a strange charm for me'. As an old man he returned to the phrase and wrote in his notebook:

> Far—far—away.
> That weird soul-phrase of something half-divine
> In earliest youth, in latest age is mine.
> Far—far—away.

Another feature of the Romantic mind began to show itself from this time. 'A kind of waking trance I have frequently had', he wrote, 'quite up from boyhood, when I have been all alone. This has generally come upon me thro' repeating my own name two or three times to myself silently, till all at once, as it were out of the intensity of the consciousness of individuality, the individuality itself seemed to dissolve and fade away into boundless being, and this was not a confused state, but the clearest of the clearest, the surest of the surest, the weirdest of the weirdest, utterly beyond words, where death was an almost laughable impossibility, the loss of personality (if so it were) seeming no extinction but the only true life'. This trance-like, exalted condition is very much the state of the Poet as Bard, the visionary singer of Truth, the 'unacknowledged legislater of the world', in Shelley's proud phrase. It was a character Tennyson maintained largely throughout his life with dignity and without affectation; we can even sense it faintly in the incantatory style of reading, still impressive through the machine-gun rattle and frying-pan sizzle of the phonograph cylinders he made in 1890.

Those cylinders are surprising relics—not merely in that they exist at all, but in the kind of voice that one hears. Surprising, at any rate, if one expected to hear the sort of sound a modern actor might make reciting *The Lotos-Eaters* or *Now Sleeps the*

Crimson Petal or *Crossing the Bar*. What we hear in fact is the sound of a powerful old man using his full voice, strong, vigorous and formidable. And there *are* surprising things about Tennyson, from first to last. How unexpected, for example, that the first sustained piece of writing that deserves its preservation should have been a three-act comedy, a verse satire that calls to mind none of Tennyson's acknowledged masters (Spenser, Milton, Keats or Shelley) as much as it does Ben Jonson. The play was called *The Devil and the Lady*. It seems he wrote it at the age of fourteen, and it is an astonishing production.

Of course there are limitations, immaturities and borrowings, but they matter surprisingly little; for as one reads, the energy and freshness become a joy. There is no mistaking that here is someone delighting in what words can do, using all the resources of his experience (books being a part of this) and finding these resources so rich and full that the images can seem to come tumbling out, apt and varied, and no self-conscious working for them. He sometimes shows off, I think, boyish and bookish in the pleasure of his control over vocabulary: 'His Tenebrious Bitumenship' is an intentionally facetious term for the devil, but also the kind of showing-off that a clever schoolboy does. Still, it would be crabby to censure a boy who has such a command of language that it sometimes bursts the seams of tight-fitting modesty and self-restraint. Admittedly, too, the joking is sometimes juvenile:

> I know a most true lover Leontio,
> That hath a nose as red as a skinned eel
> Or pickled cabbage steeped in vinegar,
> And flaming as a scarlet mailed lobster.

The Devil has just been arguing that true lovers never catch cold or get red noses because their passions generate enough warmth to keep out the cold:

>   Ay! though
> Thou had'st bolted thro' the very teeth o' the storm
> Bareheaded, every gusty drop of Heav'n
> Had run off hissing from thy glowing surface,
> As from a bar of red-hot iron.

The humour is not so very sophisticated (though there is plenty that is sillier in the Elizabethan plays he had no doubt been reading). But what liveliness of expression it provokes. How we should mark the redness of that skinned eel and the hissing of water on that hot iron bar if they had turned up in Shakespeare! And how unlikely that we should ascribe them to the young Tennyson if we were not told the identity of their author!

But the whole conception of *The Devil and the Lady* is remote from anything we would normally call Tennysonian. The play begins with the necromancer Magnus preparing to leave home and entrusting the Lady, his wife, to the care of the Devil, his 'familiar'. No sooner has he gone than various men-folk begin to arrive—a lawyer, an apothecary, a sailor and lastly a mathematician, a soldier and a monk, who come together—all suitors to the virtuous Lady. The Devil softens his voice and disguises his form sufficiently to persuade them that he is the Lady, invites them in, passes the wine around, and without having to work too hard sets them arguing against each other. In the midst of a general shemozzle Magnus returns, and then, within what must have been only a scene or two of its conclusion, the manuscript abruptly ends. This is a pity because the finished play would have been a presentable entertainment; as it is it remains a literary curiosity.

At its centre, as a plot and a comic design, are the scenes in which the Devil exposes the 'humours', vanities and absurdities of all of the suitors in turn. Antonio, the lawyer, for instance, weighs in terms of his one true love (his fees) the desire that brings him wooing the Lady:

>   the rich sound
> Of whose harmonious and most silver voice
> Steals sweeter on mine ear than does the chink
> Of golden or of silver boys* wrung out
> From the hard client's gripe—whose delicate smile
> Is worth a ten day's fee

(* Golden Boys—slang for guineas.)

The aged apothecary ('a thing of gallipots and boluses . . .

Whose hips do roll on castors, and whose love Is nauseous as his physic') is characterised in the ludicrous posture of devoted lover betrayed by bodily discomfort:

DEVIL (*as Lady*):   Art cold?
  Dost shake and shiver?
PHARMACEUTUS: Marry do I.
DEVIL: What?
  Did'st not escape the tempest?
PHARMACEUTUS: No, i' faith,
  I am half palsied with frigidity,
  I'm below zero, I am perfect ice
  Congeal'd to all intents and purposes,
  My nose, my ears, and each particular toe,
  Will quit their station—hark! my grinders chatter
  Like castanets, and pulling mills. Let's in—
  And, hark ye, some of Magnus's brown stout;
  I'll smoke a pipe of comfortable shag-tail
  By the fireside with thee. Wilt let us in?
DEVIL: Ay, presently.
PHARMACEUTUS: 'Sdeath, Madam, instantly!

The fun here is not without its sophistication, present partly in the juxtaposition of high-souled pretensions and the greedy all-too-human itch of an old man for his comforts, partly in the combination of ironical farce with the literary, scholarly associations of the Shakespearean blank-verse line. It is a kind of writing that one wishes he had it in him to develop and bring to maturity. But then, it was not in the Victorian age to value it, and *The Devil and the Lady* remained unpublished till 1930.

Other characteristics, more readily associated with the Tennyson we know, were also present in this early play. One is the pursuit of a rather misty kind of philosophical speculation. 'Are ye true substance?', asks the Devil, as he looks round him on a stormy night and wonders what reality is:

  Could the Omnipotent fill all space, if ye
  Or the least atom in ye or the least
  Division of that atom (if least can dwell
  In infinite divisibility) should be impenetrable?

I have some doubt if ye exist when none
Are by to view ye; if your Being alone
Be in the mind and the intelligence
Of the created? should some great decree
Annihilate the sentient principle
Would ye or would ye not be non-existent?
'Tis a shrewd doubt—

So it is, for a fourteen-year-old boy writing in 1823. After all,
the clever undergraduates at the beginning of E. M. Forster's
novel *The Longest Journey* are exercising their wits on much the
same problem. But I should not like to have to paraphrase the
first four lines. The lack of clarity there is due, I think, to a
muzziness of thought, and so it often was throughout his life: a
love for a kind of intuitive metaphysical ruminating, worrying
earnestly in the dark of the ancient philosophical questions about
being and non-being, man and the universe, purpose and point-
lessness. The latter particularly: whether God indeed moved in
a mysterious way, performing his wonders through real human
progress. Or whether, as the necromancer intimates, there is a
'dark reverse' of 'Life's fair tapestry':

The intertwinings and rough wanderings
Of random threads and wayward colourings—
A melée and confusion of all hues,
Disorder of a system which seemed Order.

It was a theme to which Tennyson would often return, never
expressing it more clearly and forcefully (the vividness of his
Elizabethan reading behind him) than he did as a boy.

The other characteristic that we see here and more unhesitat-
ingly recognise as Tennysonian is the descriptive power of an
essentially lyrical poet. The Elizabethanry is, after all, pastiche,
and the style that was to become his own breaks through it at
several impressive moments in the play. In this passage it is the
other way round: the mock-Shakespearean obtrudes in a strange
parenthesis through lines that are otherwise pure Tennyson:

There gleams no blue speck in the clouded waste
Of the charg'd atmosphere (not more perchance
Than is enough to make a butcher's surtout)
But minute after minute threatens us,
Lest in the misty wrappings of gray clouds
We lose the island space of narrowing blue.
The man who hoards a casket, shuddering
Will press it closer to his aching heart,
If the deep reed bed should but tremble to
The wind that strays thro' its rustling depths, or wave
Its trembling shadows to the ambiguity
Of moonlight.

Even from this time the sea counted for much in his mind. In many of the mature poems it plays a prominent part, so that it comes almost to have the force of a symbol. Here it gives rise to some of the passages which have the most personal poetic feeling:

The mighty waste of moaning waters lay
So goldenly in moonlight, whose clear lamp
With its long line of vibratory lustre
Trembled on the dun surface, that my spirit
Was buoyant with rejoicings.

Possibly it is a sentimental intrusion to let anything one happens to know about the artist influence one's judgement of the work. These lines are good ones whoever they were written by, but I must confess to being moved by the knowledge of the poet's extreme youth. Juvenilia are not always so engaging, are often extremely embarrassing for author and reader alike. Among those I would want to see preserved, *The Devil and the Lady* and a few other early poems of Tennyson would have an assured place.

It is interesting that the *Poems by Two Brothers* seems to contain the least memorable examples of his early work. This was Tennyson's first publication. A local publisher brought it out in 1826 and it achieved a fair success. The *Gentleman's Magazine* found the poems 'full of amiable feelings, expressed for the most part with elegance and correctness'. This was perhaps part of the trouble, for they read to us very like literary exercises, skilful but conventional. Of the one-hundred-and-three poems, Alfred is known to have written forty-two. Three or four were by Frederick; the principal collaborator was Charles. Sir Charles Tennyson comments: 'One can trace the subjects and the methods of almost all [the poems] to the Somersby library and very little to Alfred's personal experience'.

More impressive are the 'unpublished' early poems which Sir Charles edited in 1931. A few are also included in the first volume of the *Memoir* by Hallam Tennyson, who quotes Dr. Jowett, the great Master of Balliol and a close friend of Tennyson in later life: 'They are most original and it is wonderful how the whelp could have known such things'. The varied references and the wide vocabulary of *The Devil and the Lady* may be what Jowett had chiefly in mind. This is an objective, out-going kind of knowledge, however, whereas the individual poems show already a depth of feeling and the kind of knowledge that emotional experience brings with it. Already he understood the pain of loss. Dreams bring back—

> sunny faces of lost days
> Long to mouldering dust consign'd,
> Forms which live but to the mind.

In sleep the lost joy is recaptured, but all too briefly, for the lips and eyes fade:

> And the hollow dark I dread
> Closes round my friendless head
>
> And far away, to left and right,
> Whirlwinds waste the dizzy night,
> And I lie and toss and mourn,
> Hopeless, heartless and forlorn.

With the rhyme and the tidy balance of the lines, these sorrows find a neatness of expression which may seem to belie their truth. When he allows images to speak for him, however, the verse rings true: the turbulence of troubled sleep is finely rendered in 'whirlwinds waste the dizzy night', and the vacancy left by the vanishing of a dream's brightness is caught in 'the hollow dark I dread'. Darkness sometimes troubles and sometimes comforts in these poems, but it is a recurrent presence. In *Perdidi Diem* it comes as the gloom of his own soul:

> but th' eternal mystic lamp,
> Lighting that charnel damp,
> Wounding with dreadful days that solid gloom,
> Making a 'darkness visible'

One often wonders why the unhappiness that he must have known in his boyhood at Somersby does not dominate these early poems. In this one it does; but what remains the remarkable thing and the sign of real strength is that in general the self-indulgent melancholy we might have expected is so rare. The young poet looks constantly at things outside the self, with a keen sense of beauty and a flexible, experimental, live way with the art he is learning.

When, in a part of the poem called *Armageddon*, he does look at himself, it is with exultation:

> I felt my soul grow godlike, and my spirit
> With supernatural excitation bound
> Within me, and my mental eye grew large
> With such a vast circumference of thought,
> That, in my vanity, I seem'd to stand
> Upon the outward verge and bound alone
> Of God's omniscience. Each failing sense
> As with a momentary flash of light,
> Grew thrillingly distinct and keen. I saw
> The smallest grain that dappled the dark Earth,
> The indistinctest atom in deep air,
> The Moon's white cities, and the opal width
> Of her small, glowing lakes, her silver heights
> Unvisited with dew or vagrant cloud,
> And the unsounded, undescended depth
> Of her black hollows. Nay—the hum of men
> Or other things talking in unknown tongues,
> And notes of busy life in distant worlds,
> Beat, like a far wave, on my anxious ear.

I wonder'd with deep wonder at myself:
My mind seem'd wing'd with knowledge and the strength
Of holy musings and immense Ideas,
Even to Infinitude. All sense of Time
And Being and Place was swallowed up and lost
Within a victory of boundless thought.
I was a part of the Unchangeable,
A scintillation of Eternal Mind,
Remix'd and burning with its parent fire.
Yea! in that hour I could have fallen down
Before my own strong soul and worshipp'd it.

Sir Charles Tennyson believes that the poet was fifteen when he
wrote *Armageddon*. The literary influences are very obvious, as
they were in *The Devil and the Lady*: *Armageddon* is Miltonic
and takes itself very seriously. But the vision, the mystical
elevation of spirit, speak with the authority of a personal truth.
Again one is moved partly by the thought of the 'young whelp'
whose art could already take the pressure of such knowledge
and such emotions. But again the recognition is tinged with a
regretful irony. For as the high-spirited, un-pedestrian comedy
of *The Devil and the Lady* is unmatched in Tennyson's later
work, so that fresh, strong exultancy expressed in the passage
from *Armageddon* is another quality lost to the mature poet.
Both these works were excluded from the published *Poems by
Two Brothers* because they were, as Hallam Tennyson put it,
'too much out of the common for the public taste'. Tennyson
was always responsive to public taste and sensitive to criticism
('Hope nourishes Youth and Poesy, Abuse represses and
injures them' is the translation of a Latin tag inscribed on one of
his first notebooks). The gains accruing from such responsive-
ness no doubt included the Laureateship and the status he enjoyed in his lifetime as the Poet of his age, a status increasingly
confirmed (not necessarily as a compliment) in this century. But
the public taste of the nineteenth century was not entirely
favourable to the growth of a poet; and it brought its losses, too.

3

Cambridge

'Something like Hyperion . . . with a pipe in
his mouth' (Edward Fitzgerald)

Alfred and Charles went up to Cambridge in November 1827.
Frederick was there already, with a considerable reputation as a
scholar and an absentee from Chapel. He had moved from St.
John's to Trinity, so now all three Tennysons were at the same
college. This did not guarantee, as it might have done, a friendly
and happy Freshman's year for Alfred, and at first he appears
to have been miserably homesick. *The Outcast*, a poem written
before going up to the University, shows that he had felt even
then how much the loss of his home would mean, and how
painfully 'Memory's widowed eyes' would recall absent forms
in 'sunless days'. At Cambridge he wrote, as perhaps others
have done, a poem called *Home*, and in his letters he complained
sadly of his loneliness. He also complained about the University.
'When, my dearest Aunt, may I hope to see you again? I know
not how it is, but I feel isolated here in the midst of society. The
country is so disgustingly level, the revelry of the place so
monotonous, the studies of the University so uninteresting, so
much matter of fact. None but dry-headed, calculating, angular
little gentlemen can take much delight in them.' Later he found
acceptance, friendship and great happiness, and in *In Memoriam*
(LXXXVII) he could write with affection of 'the reverend walls
In which of old I wore the gown'. But his criticisms remain.
Between tutor and pupil there was 'a great gulf fixed', and, more
telling still, 'There was a lack of love in Cambridge then'. His

26

Lines on Cambridge of 1830, unpublished till after his death, are still impressive:

> Therefore your Halls, your ancient Colleges,
> Your portals statued with old kings and queens,
> Your gardens, myriad-volumed libraries,
> Wax-lighted chapels, and rich carven screens,
> Your doctors, and your proctors, and your deans,
> Shall not avail you, when the Day-beam sports
> New-risen o'er awaken'd Albion. No!
> Nor yet your solemn organ-pipes that blow
> Melodious thunders thro' your vacant courts
> At noon and eve, because your manner sorts
> Not with this age wherefrom ye stand apart,
> Because the lips of little children preach
> Against you, you that do profess to teach
> And teach us nothing, feeding not the heart.

The University, he held, had a responsibility to its age, and this it was not fulfilling. Its students too had an obligation not to 'stand apart' but to involve themselves seriously in the world around them. This was also the doctrine of a group called 'The Apostles'. Its members included John Kemble, Richard Chenevix Trench, Richard Monckton Milnes, James Spedding, Henry Lushington, W. H. Thompson, W. H. Brookfield, Charles Merivale and later Arthur Hallam. These became Tennyson's great friends; remarkable men all of them, and a company both genial and intelligent. Their influence on Tennyson was great.

Whether it was beneficial is another matter. Sir Harold Nicolson in his book on Tennyson thinks not, and he speaks of 'one's inevitable dislike' of the society. The title of 'The Apostles' had been bestowed in satire on what was originally a fairly informal discussion group; it was accepted part in humour, part in earnest, for they knew they had a gospel for mankind and did not much doubt their fitness as evangelists. Of course there grew up, as one of the members said years afterwards, 'an immense self-conceit'. There was also an earnestness, a sense of mission that could become priggish, prim and pompous. And one cannot say that this is not the dominant impression 'one'

27

receives in reading about them, because for Sir Harold Nicolson it is. The society was nevertheless one of the best things the University had to offer to its members. 'From the "Apostles" I, at least, learned to think as a *free man*', said John Kemble. They thought about matters philosophical, political, moral and aesthetic. Three of the subjects for discussion are recorded in Hallam Tennyson's *Memoir*: 'Have Shelley's poems an immoral tendency?' (Tennyson voted 'No'); 'Is an intelligible First Cause deducible from the phenomenon of the Universe?' (Tennyson rather more interestingly voted 'No'); and 'Is there any rule of moral action beyond general expediency?' ('Aye'). Perhaps it is all rather funny and grandiose and over-serious: Sir Harold's tone implies that he thinks so and that he would have liked them better if they had mixed with the lads who 'crash'd the glass and beat the floor', as *In Memoriam* has it. But then, intellectual interests, refinement of taste, and even 'earnestness' are not such bad things to find at a university. And it was not all so serious anyway. The Apostles were not ponderous, humourless people. Most of them—Spedding, Milnes and Kemble, for instance—were high-spirited, readily likeable men. Brookfield particularly had inexhaustible wit and inventiveness: 'He was far the most amusing man I ever met or ever shall meet,' said W. H. Thompson. It is the sort of pronouncement we greet with scepticism, but the account rings true. Even Tennyson contributed to the light entertainment. He could imitate George IV or 'with his mop of hair spread out around his great head, he would impersonate the sun coming out from a cloud and returning into one again'.

The society was, moreover, a timely creation. 'Your manner sorts Not with this age wherefrom ye stand apart'. So Tennyson had written in his indictment of Cambridge. 'This age' was one in which thoughtful men had plenty to think about. In the front of their minds would be a concern about the ideals of the French Revolution, the frightful history of the Terror, the Revolutionary and Napoleonic wars, the triumphant ultra-conservatism of the Vienna Congress, the distress in England with the Luddite riots and the growing blackness of the new industrial towns, the issue of Catholic Emancipation, and the inflammatory cause of parliamentary reform. Liberalism and new knowledge stirred many a stagnant water. The poetry of Byron and Shelley put fire in many a heart that felt itself waiting for the spark from heaven. The Apostles responded to these calls, which indeed amounted exactly to the need to think, in Kemble's phrase, 'as a free man'. So Tennyson, along with the others, supported the Anti-Slavery Convention and looked eagerly to Europe for the cracking of old despotisms. 'The warrens of the poor' (the phrase comes from one of his very last poems, *Locksley Hall Sixty Years After*), the 'Condition of the People' question, were not matters of indifference to him; and though rioting and popular agitation horrified him, he nevertheless rejoiced with all his being at the passing of the Reform Bill in 1832. The news of this event reached Somersby in the middle of the night and the whole Tennyson family went out into the darkness and rang the church bells for all they were worth. To this joy in a good cause the Liberalism of the Apostles had no doubt contributed.

New ideas were abroad in other than social and political matters. The conservatism of the Church was assailed, and we find Tennyson also supporting the idea that the clergy need not be committed to a belief in all the Thirty-Nine Articles. In Cambridge the religious establishment still reflected the teaching of William Paley, who had preached eighteenth-century deism, with its chilly, impersonal God, so very much at odds with the live being, the 'eternal mind', to which young Tennyson (and Wordsworth before him) had felt so close. It was an honorary member of the Apostles, Connop Thirlwall, who did most to bring warmth and intelligence into the religious life of Cambridge. A Fellow of Trinity, he made a strong appeal to men like Tennyson, just as, by adopting liberal causes like the admission of religious dissenters, he made enemies among the University authorities. For it was dangerous in those times to voice any kind of unorthodoxy in religion. F. D. Maurice, one of the founders of the Apostles, had to resign from King's College, London, in 1853, having published his belief that the doctrine of eternal punishment for the wicked in hell-fire was an unchristian superstitition. W. H. Brookfield, then a popular preacher in London, forfeited his chances of promotion in the Church by suggesting that Christ was not necessarily tempted in the wilderness by the devil in actual bodily form. And John Kemble, another of the Apostles, nearly lost his degree through writing of the still venerated Paley as a 'miserable sophist'.

So I am not sure that 'one's dislike' of the Apostles is so 'inevitable'. Nor even that, as Nicolson suggests, they had such a bad effect on Tennyson by insisting on the importance of the poet's 'message', rather than on his true reason for existence as a creator of beautiful things. They hoped that he would be able to do both: to write about things that mattered, and still write beautifully. In any case, the advice was to come from plenty of other quarters during the next decade or so. Whatever 'played such havoc with his later compositions' (Nicolson's phrase) was deep in the character of the nineteenth century, and was not the particular fault of his Cambridge friends. The only way he could have escaped such influences would have been by staying in Lincolnshire (which is what Edward Fitzgerald said he should have done). Had he done so he would not have been The Victorian Poet we know. There would have been profit and loss; and the loss would have included *In Memoriam*, for he would not have met Arthur Hallam.

Hallam was Tennyson's closest friend. His sudden death in 1833 was the greatest shock and grief of Tennyson's life and it inspired what is possibly his finest single work. Hallam was a young man of extraordinary brilliance. A prodigious scholar as a child (he could read French and Latin fluently at the age of nine and had already written several tragedies), he vastly impressed his contemporaries at Eton, amongst whom, said one of them, 'he stood supreme'. That 'one' was Gladstone, who in his memoirs described how Hallam's friends felt themselves 'at once bound closely to him by commanding affection, and left far behind by the rapid, full and rich development of his ever-searching brain'. He was blessed with a comfortable home and a respected father, a charming manner, a fine complexion, an 'angelic radiance' (according to Fanny Kemble), and remarkable eloquence. Everyone agreed with Tennyson that 'he was as near perfection as mortal man could be' and that he would have been known as a great man had he lived. Perhaps one should again refer to Sir Harold Nicolson's account for a different way of looking at Hallam, for he clearly finds so much perfection irritating. Hallam's poems and letters are not so wonderfully intelligent as all that, he points out. He notices also that his friends 'were not quite sure what [his] future was to be, certain only that it would be rich and meteoric'. Tennyson saw him as a great statesman, not a great poet. 'With this conception it was Gladstone who disagreed; for him it was as a writer on theological and religious subjects that Hallam would fulfil his destiny. But on the main point—on the point of his eventual and blazing success—their agreement was remarkable.' The urbane manner of the critic belittles subtly, in a manner no doubt learnt from Lytton Strachey's way with other eminent Victorians; but the observation is shrewd enough and its implications may well be just.

For Tennyson the friendship of Arthur Hallam lightened a darkening existence as only a very rare affection could have done. One of the unpublished sonnets written during his time at Cambridge expresses his feeling of comfort amid the depression that would still assail him. He sees himself 'all sin-sickened, loathing my disgrace', able still to find 'a shadow and a resting place in thee'. Hallam is not named but there can be little doubt that the poem was addressed to him. He supplied some of the clear needs of Tennyson's nature: a stability and (for all his exceptional gifts) a normality to put against the moodily neurotic strain that Tennyson found in himself, a sunny disposition to offset the 'blackbloodedness'. Perhaps some vague kind of social yearning found satisfaction too, for Tennyson with his northern accent and his dirty shirts ('Which Tennyson? The slovenly one?', was a question once asked) was not readily and conventionally acceptable, while Arthur Hallam lent evident grace to any company he joined. Above all came the need of a passionate nature for close understanding with another. Hallam, in spite of the good luck he had enjoyed through most of his young life, had known unhappiness enough to be responsive and sympathetic, and in him Tennyson felt that he had found something 'passing the love of women'; for women, at this time in his life, seem to have been somewhat remote beings, subjects for gallantry and graceful portraits in verse, but hardly for the full kind of human relationship that in Hallam he desired and got.

Hallam also helped Tennyson to gain some much-needed self-confidence. Each, in fact, said very gratifying things about the other, and Hallam, writing to Gladstone, gave it as his opinion that Tennyson promised fair 'to be the greatest poet of our generation, perhaps of our century'. Not that he was the only one to be impressed. Tennyson had very quickly made a mark in Cambridge, almost in spite of himself. His appearance alone made it difficult for him to pass unnoticed. 'That man must be a poet,' W. H. Thompson, one of the Apostles, said when he first saw him. 'Six feet high, broad-chested, strong-limbed, his face Shakespearean, with deep eyelids, his forehead ample, crowned with dark wavy hair, his head finely poised, his hand the admiration of sculptors, long fingers with square tips, soft as a child's but of great size and strength. What struck one most about him was the union of strength with refinement': so runs the account of a friend quoted in Hallam Tennyson's *Memoir*. Then there was the famous voice: 'like the sound of a pinewood,' Carlyle described it. His normal reticence left him when he read; and with his deep voice and his rhythmic style he achieved an overpoweringly emotional and dramatic effect. '*Oriana* Tennyson used to repeat in a way not to be forgotten at Cambridge tables', said Fitzgerald, who also left a vivid picture of his appearance: 'Something like Hyperion shorn of his beams in Keats' poem; with a pipe in his mouth'.

One gets the impression that these were largely happy years. A world outside Somersby and self had been encountered. It had offered good things to him and had recognised good things in him. Among the tokens of this esteem was the Chancellor's Medal which Tennyson won in 1829 for a poem called *Timbuctoo*. Tennyson did not choose the title; it was the subject set. But into it he found he could put some of his boyhood poem *Armageddon*, and though the verses were thought obscure and eccentric, they were very clearly the work of a true poet. One of the Apostles wrote to his father, 'Tennyson's poem has made quite a sensation; it is certainly equal to most parts of Milton'. There was also a first involvement in international affairs. In 1830 a number of Spaniards, refugees from the despotic rule of Ferdinand VII, decided they wanted to go back. One of the Apostles heard of this and several of them, Hallam and Tennyson included, took up the cause. A boat was provided and after a number of difficulties the Spaniards set off. The King objected to having rebels in his country under British protection, however, and eventually they were caught and killed. One Englishman died with them (not an Apostle), and Hallam and Tennyson who had been on a special liaison mission to other rebels in the Pyrenees came home thrilled about the scenery and disillusioned about the rebellion.

All through this period there was a plentiful supply of poetry. Most of it appeared in the 1830 volume called *Poems, chiefly lyrical*. By the next year Hyperion and his pipe were no longer to be seen in Cambridge, though memories remained along with a loyal interest in his career. And in 1832, no later, the Union was debating the question 'Tennyson or Milton, which the greater poet?'.

4

Poems: 1830, 1832 and 1842

'A respectable show of blossom' (William Wordsworth)

The fifty-six poems published in 1830 (*Poems, chiefly lyrical*) were fruits of Tennyson's years at Cambridge. In December 1832 a further collection of thirty poems appeared in a volume dated 1833 and often referred to as belonging to that year. There followed ten years' silence, in which only two short pieces reminded the public of Tennyson's existence. Then came the book of 1842, containing thirty-six new poems with earlier poems reprinted, many of them revised.

Out of these hundred-and-thirty-odd poems, some read essentially as exercises in a literary manner, some are irritating, some sentimental; others are pleasant yet leave no lasting impression. Most readers would probably be happy with an anthology of about twenty-five, and I daresay there would not be a great deal of disagreement about what was to be included and what left out. In this present section, I propose to take ten poems from the three volumes, hoping to show with them something of the area in which Tennyson's mind was working in this period and something of the directions in which his art was developing.

Let us put a question with only a very personal, subjective answer. If you had to select a single poem to illustrate what you mean by 'Tennysonian', what would you choose? For me it would be *Mariana*, from the poems of 1830; or, at least, it would be in my mind as a strong contender. If I had never seen it and had been given it to identify, I think there would have been no question at all about its authorship, and I should also have felt,

34

'Ah yes, it's *this* that is home to him; this is what at first he wanted to express, and later it was precisely what he did *not* want to express, for he knew his duty and was a conscientious man: but this is what is at the heart of him'. Not that he himself *is* Mariana, with her frustration, her listlessness and death-wish, but that this sense of beauty in desolation was what as a poet he had most personally and effectively to express. So many other sides of him exist and find expression, yet so many of them were 'attitudes': sincerely held and honestly cultivated, but things that he thought he ought to do, interests he ought to have, feelings he ought to try to inculcate. Many voices, too, that he felt he ought to speak in: the fiery tones of a Shelley, the organ voice of a Milton, the simple, dignified tongue of the Bible. But in *Mariana* the feeling is native to him, and the voice is always his own.

Mariana is the full expression of a feeling which repeatedly enters other poems in this early volume. The *Leonine Elegiacs* has it, with its melancholy landscape:

> Sadly the far kine loweth; the glimmering water outfloweth.

Or the *Song* beginning 'A Spirit haunts the year's last hours':

> The air is damp, and hush'd, and close,
> As a sick man's room when he taketh repose
> An hour before death;
> My very heart faints and my whole soul grieves
> At the moist smell of the rotting leaves
>   . . . and the year's last rose.

Or the rather more sentimental lyric, *My Life is full of weary days*. In *The Dying Swan*, Tennyson has something of the desolation of Sibelius' lonely *cor anglais* in *The Swan of Tuonela*:

> Ever the weary wind went on,
> And took the reed-tops as it went.

The word which again and again evokes this music is 'weary'. It is there bringing the true Tennyson into the poem called *Nothing will die*:

> When will the stream be aweary of flowing
> > Under my eye?
> When will the wind be aweary of blowing
> > Over the sky?

Always when the verse comes to life with marked feeling and individuality it is at this evocation of a landscape whose grey, lonely beauty matches a strange, hollow yearning in the human being. The scene and mood are one, and in *Mariana* they match as perfectly as in any poem written.

Tennyson is working a poet's peculiar kind of magic: he throws out a series of pictures, lantern-slides upon a screen, and what takes shape as we watch them is something quite different; for the dying day, the level waste, the shrill winds and the poplar trees come to be experienced by us as they are by her, and the pictures show us as clearly as anything her frustration and dreariness.

This is a kind of poetry most *un*like the following lines, taken from a poem called *Isabel*, which happens to be printed in the collected edition on the page opposite *Mariana*:

> The intuitive decision of a bright
> > And thorough-edged intellect to part
> > Error from crime.

Contrast the opening of *Mariana*:

> With blackest moss the flower-pots
> > Were thickly crusted, one and all:
> The rusted nails fell from the knots
> > That held the pear to the gable-wall.

In both poems the prime purpose is to show us a woman. Now the way of showing us Mariana could have been quite different. The first lines might have read:

> The long-accustomed carelessness of a dulled
> > And unavailing decadence to tend
> > Abundance with firm hand.

This is bloodless and stiff-jointed, and I don't suppose that

Tennyson could have written anything so bad. But *Mariana*, though it looks like mood-music and appears non-intellectual, does *mean* something, and it could have been written in this explicit and abstract way. Instead it works by image and symbol, so that emotion and understanding are enriched together. Thus we know, without being told in so many words, that the kind of purposefulness and energy that maintain standards has gone out of this life, that its isolation is complete ('Unlifted was the clinking latch'), and that a darkness of time without event has come upon it like a featureless landscape and an endless night:

> After the flitting of the bats,
> > When thickest dark did trance the sky,
> > She drew her casement-curtain by,
> And glanced athwart the glooming flats.

The refrain ('I am aweary') is certainly explicit enough, but otherwise the expression is oblique. Incidental details come to have the representative force of symbols only in a very unobtrusive, unforced way. Thus, there is a poplar tree, 'all silver-green with gnarled bark', growing alone on the level waste. It is mentioned again in the next verse:

> But when the moon was very low,
> > And wild winds bound within their cell,
> > The shadow of the poplar fell
> Upon her bed, across her brow.

And again in the last verse:

> > the sound
> Which to the wooing wind aloof
> The poplar made

The erotic associations here are lightly, subtly handled, both pointed and poignant in their restraint. For the gnarled bark suggests a maleness the woman will never embrace; the insubstantiality of shadows is all that falls upon her bed; and the sterility of wind moving the branches of a tree is all the reality that love can ever have as it moves in the frustrated desires of her mind.

'I am half sick of shadows' is the cry of another of Tennyson's women. In *The Lady of Shalott* we have another isolated life, and again we know her and feel with her largely by a process of transference and suggestion. Two passionate statements are all the direct, face-to-face knowledge we have of her, yet her feelings are the vivid centre of this poem as Mariana's are of the other.

The poem constantly moves inward to what we call the heart: through the spacious expanse of field, road and sky it penetrates further and further till it reaches the innermost nerve, the microscopic seat of the emotions, the centre of a power which for the individual can transform the whole exterior world. For Mariana, the beauty around her is poisoned by what is within her; for the Lady of Shalott, life is at first well enough. 'She lives with little joy or fear', says the original version of the poem. So, 'living and partly-living', in Eliot's phrase, existing in a kind of limbo, she observes the world at a second-remove and at least comes to no harm. But the reality that is borne in upon her is a recognition of her abnormality, a recognition that other people have something she has not:

> Or when the moon was overhead,
> Came two young lovers lately wed;
> 'I am half sick of shadows', said
>   The Lady of Shalott.

So again, as with Mariana, a pressure of frustration grows until it bursts as suddenly and uncontrollably as Sir Lancelot flashes into the crystal mirror.

Here too then, in *The Lady of Shalott*, is a core of thought and understanding. It is not a matter of a 'message' or a 'hidden significance', these overused and inappropriate terms that suggest the reader has to 'do' a work of art as he might a crossword puzzle, looking for clues to some mystery that the author has cunningly worked in and hidden somewhere or other. It is simply a matter of reading the poem, a process from which the Victorians themselves seem in an odd way to have drawn back. Some comments in *The Times* of 12 October, 1848, possibly by the father of Gerard Manley Hopkins, are representative: 'It is pure, sensuous poetry. We forbear to ask too closely what hidden meanings dwell in its misty dreaminess. We would not for the world break our toy to discover its concealed music.' But the analogy is a false one: you do not destroy anything by reading fully, unless it be a false, meretricious appeal that should be rejected anyway. Yet it is interesting that the Victorians should have withdrawn from a full reading, for at the heart of this poem as of *Mariana* is a sexual frustration whose force the nineteenth century did all it could to disguise or ignore. It is also interesting that they were perpetually asking Tennyson for poetry with a message, something meaningful and relevant to the problems of their time, and not merely a beautiful toy. In *Mariana* and *The Lady of Shalott* he had in fact given something meaningful; but incomplete reading somehow meant that you could say 'sensuous poetry' about them, think that you had thereby appreciated them, and be quite untouched by the thought and feeling that were at the heart of them. Thus Tennyson was influenced little by little to write with greater explicitness or with a more formalised, allegorical method, and to choose subjects from which his reason told him the people of his own time could learn. This sets the condition for a calculated kind of verse; and while Tennyson's later poetry has many excellences, I think that it only rarely catches the power he had in his youth to fuse image, sound and idea so that the one *was* the other.

The Lady of Shalott, then, is not an allegory, though, as in *Mariana*, the images sometimes have the power of symbols. The mirror, for instance, suggests much beyond its role as an item in a fairy story. For as the Lady weaves 'the mirror's magic sights' in her tapestry she is herself partly taking the role of the artist, and her existence in the island castle has something in common with the artist's apartness. Moreover, as she sees reality only through her mirror, so the artist may tend to experience vicariously, drawing his knowledge not from direct contact but from other works of art. He has his own special nature, like the Lady; partly an affliction to him, this sense of difference, partly a blessing and possibly the very condition of his being an artist at all. For life in the ordinary day-to-day world he may be all unfit, as was the Lady, and, for him as for her, only disaster may follow the attempt to break bounds. This is not 'the message' of *The Lady of Shalott*, but it is, I think, a part of the ground out of which the poem grew.

Another poem grew in ground nearby, less fertile, but still rich, natural soil. The issue here is defined. There is an explicit concern with the predicament of the artist; and the method, explicitly stated in the first line, is 'a sort of allegory'. This explicitness makes *The Palace of Art* a less richly suggestive poem than *The Lady of Shalott*, but it is still an interesting and memorable one.

It tells of the attempt to create a special world of beauty and knowledge, sufficient to satisfy the soul of a sensitive thoughtful man, a world both delightful and secure:

> . . . I built it firm. Of ledge or shelf
> The rock rose clear, or winding stair.
> My soul would live alone unto herself
>   In her high palace there.

Just as the Lady of Shalott saw reality and yet was isolated and protected from it, so should the soul in its Palace of Art take cognizance of everything and be involved in nothing. 'All these are mine', it will say:

> And let the world have peace or wars,
>   'Tis one to me.

Art, after all, has within its scope the sum total of man's experience, or the best part of it. Poetry has been written 'fit for every mood And change of my still soul'. Paintings have been painted showing every scene one can wish for. There is also Philosophy ('not less than Truth') and Religion ('not less than Life'). The great artists and thinkers are 'my gods, with whom I dwell', and there is the additional pleasure of feeling how lucky and superior one is to have their company rather than that of the Philistines who over-populate the real world:

> O God-like isolation which art mine,
>   I can but count thee perfect gain,

> What time I watch the darkening droves of swine
> > That range on yonder plain.

But the allegory has further to go. Trouble comes, and with it a moral. For this isolation brings its punishment and the soul begins to suffer:

> God, before whom ever lie bare
> The abysmal deeps of Personality,
> > Plagued her with sore despair.

The soul becomes, as we would say, neurotic, depressed by the stagnation of its existence:

> And death and life she hated equally.

So the soul leaves her palace, takes instead a cottage in the outside world, hoping to come back perhaps when the guilt of this unnatural and irresponsible way of life is purged: coming back, moreover, 'with others'. We then return to the Preface for the explicit moral. The love of Beauty by and for itself is 'a glorious Devil':

> And he that shuts Love out, in turn shall be
> Shut out from Love.

This Preface to *The Palace of Art* is headed *To—*. The blank was meant for Tennyson's friend R. C. Trench, one of the Apostles and later Archbishop of Canterbury. In their Trinity days, Trench had said to him, 'Tennyson, we cannot live by art'. The weighty words went home and became the starting point of *The Palace of Art*. The poem, of course, comes down in decisive agreement with Trench's dictum, but it presents that conclusion as the outcome of a struggle in which the battle-ground is the soul. For us nowadays, it may possibly be difficult to see this struggle as a very real thing, though seen in general terms the dilemma is recognisably modern and universal. There is a will in all of us to go off and enjoy ourselves in our own way. This is constantly being checked by our recognition that we are members of a society, that we have duties towards this, and that in the long run it will probably be best for us to involve ourselves in our fellow men rather than cut adrift and do just as we please. So much is Speech-Day platitude, but it may be true and important all the same. The particular form that the dilemma took for Tennyson involved the whole question of his function as an artist, and it also reflects a division of opinion and practice which, like a deep crack in a picture, went right through the nineteenth century. Tennyson turned his back on the Palace of Art, but others found it an increasingly attractive residence. From the eighteen-thirties on, the 'aesthetic' movement grew, cultivating Beauty as an end in itself, holding (with Oscar Wilde) that art served no 'practical' purpose, and most emphatically denying that the artist had anything whatsoever to do with morality. If, when his friend Trench said, 'Tennyson, we cannot live by art', Tennyson had answered, 'Oh yes we can and I'm going to try', we should now find him on the other side of the crack in our picture of the nineteenth century. *The Palace of Art*, if it had been written at all, would then have been a vindication of art-for-art's-sake aestheticism rather than the picturesque Morality poem that it is. Tennyson would not have become Poet Laureate and he would not have written the *Idylls of the King*. He might have made masterpieces, and later ages would certainly have seen him as a more colourful figure than he now appears. But, as it was, he agreed with his friend Trench. And most of us, no doubt, would have done the same.

The Palace of Art, then, apart from its poetic worth, is a document very central to the development of Tennyson's mind and art. Yet the poem simply makes explicit a process that would be clear to us even if it had not been written. Its main preoccupations recur in several other important poems. The conflict between a sense of responsibility and the desire to take one's pleasure and one's ease at will is also represented in *The Lotos-Eaters*, that famous anthology piece where the beauty of image and sound almost disguise the fact that the poem is *about* something. In this we are to suppose that Ulysses' sailors, weary 'of action and of motion', have come to an island where all the conditions for an easy, untroubled existence seem to be present, and where any qualms of conscience about the rightness of so much relaxation can be allayed by eating the lotos plant which the 'mild-eyed, melancholy' inhabitants offer. The drug works its spell and the sailors abandon all ambition to return to their homes:

> Surely, surely, slumber is more sweet than toil, the shore
> Than labour in the deep mid-ocean, wind and wave and oar;
> Oh rest ye, brother mariners, we will not wander more.

Living with the lotos-eaters or in the Palace of Art evidently has this in common—that the soul lives 'alone unto itself' and neglects all social responsibility. The causes, art or beauty on the one hand and a drug on the other, might appear to be very different things. But in Tennyson's conception they are interestingly alike. The lotos opens a way to pure beauty; and pure beauty, whether of art or nature, in turn acts as a drug or an intoxicant to the spirit. As the lotos-drug works its spell so there comes (as in the working of mescalin as Aldous Huxley describes it) a heightened perception of beauty:

> There is sweet music here that softer falls
> Than petals from blown roses on the grass,
> Or night-dews on still waters between walls
> Of shadowy granite, in a gleaming pass;
> Music that gentlier on the spirit lies
> Than tired eyelids upon tired eyes.

When the soul, in *The Palace of Art*, describes the appeal of art, we recognise that it is essentially thinking of art as an intoxicant:

> So that she thought, 'And who shall gaze upon
>   My palace with unblinded eyes,
> While this great bow will waver in the sun,
>   And that sweet incense rise?'

This is the Romantic speaking: the 'sweet incense' of art will drug the destructive, analytical, conscious mind and will work a magic, exalting the spirit. The psalmist spoke of 'Wine that maketh glad the heart of man' and the Romantics found Beauty a more satisfying intoxicant. Keats makes the point in *Ode to a Nightingale*. He will achieve exaltation of spirit, he says:

> Not charioted by Bacchus and his pards,
> But on the viewless wings of Poesy

On the whole, our present age is not one that uses art for intoxication. 'Religion is the opium of the people,' says the famous Marxist tag; between the two World Wars the various political 'isms' were powerful intoxicants; nowadays, so Malcolm Muggeridge tell us, the opium of the people is sex. The Romantics who achieved this exaltation, submitting their normal restraints to the power of art and beauty, had found better masters than most. But drugs, however artistic and beautiful, are still habit-forming, and a lifetime's submission, easy and attractive for a poet to fall into, would be both a perversion and a cheat. Keats recognises this at the end of *Ode to a Nightingale*, and Tennyson is recognising it in *The Lotos-Eaters*. One can tell, nevertheless, that the attraction is still potent.

In fact, it is only by putting *The Lotos-Eaters* back into its context as a nineteenth-century poem with Tennyson as its author, that one sees it as a denunciation at all. It *is* that, in intention: it exposes the power of a temptation, one that is particularly insidious because it induces a habit, and because the intellect can think up a whole chain of reasoning by which to defend the indulgence. But the poem contains not a word of reproach or of moralising (it is all the stronger as a poem for that). The whole creation of feeling, image and thought is so complete and, in the literal sense, sympathetic, that one knows the author felt the pull of this escapism with abnormal acuteness. All his sense of beauty is engaged in rendering the drugged state of the lotos-eaters:

> Here are cool mosses deep,
> And thro' the moss the ivies creep,
> And in the stream the long-leaved flowers weep,
> And from the craggy ledge the poppy hangs in sleep.

All his powers of reasoning, moreover, are engaged in constructing the defence. Man, he argues, is supposedly 'the roof and crown of things', the highest form of created life; yet he is condemned to a life of toil. This, he says, is not simply the way of nature. Look at other forms of life well below us in the scale of life as we normally rate it. Trees and fruits, for example: they ripen, fade, and fall, having 'their allotted length of days'. But for us:

> Blight and famine, plague and earthquake,
> > roaring deeps and fiery sands,
> Clanging fights, and flaming towns, and
> > sinking ships, and praying hands.

We are required to do battle with evil; this is supposed to be the will of the gods. But what is the nature of the gods themselves? Why, surely, they can only be like us as we are now, reclining on the hills, sipping their nectar and caring nothing for mankind. For (so goes the argument) how can they be responsible, benevolent and active on mankind's behalf, when the world is so full of miseries which they do nothing to remedy?

> . . . they smile, they find a music centred
> > in a doleful song
> Steaming up, a lamentation and an ancient tale of wrong,
> Like a tale of little meaning tho' the words are strong;
> Chanted from an ill-used race of men that cleave the soil,
> Sow the seed, and reap the harvest with enduring toil,
> Storing yearly little dues of wheat, and wine and oil:
> Till they perish, and they suffer—some, 'tis whispered—
> > down in hell
> Suffer endless anguish, others in Elysian valleys dwell,
> Resting weary limbs at last on beds of asphodel.

In all this Tennyson is looking at 'the human condition'. Because he is writing under the guise of pre-Christian sailors who have 'gone wrong', he can give voice to an interpretation of life that calls into question all the cheerful God's-in-his-heaven-all's-right-with-the-world outlook that was especially dear to the people of his own time. He can even question the nature of the Power in heaven that has ordered life in such a fashion. Tennyson never thought harder than he did in this poem. The fact that so much imagination, thought and feeling goes into the expression of *this* suggests, surely, a division within Tennyson himself. *Officially* he is writing a denunciation; *creatively* he is making a defence. The good Christian in him has urged him perpetually to believe that life and its creator are good, and that he himself must play his humble but God-given part in making life better. The other side of his nature saw in life 'a lamentation and an ancient tale of wrong' over which a good God could not preside; it urged him personally away from all commitment, towards the enjoyment of peace and beauty in which alone he could find certain good.

This same division is to some extent reflected in *The Two Voices*. In this the poet argues within himself on the question whether life is worth living. We are to suppose that in a sleepless night and in a mood of intense depression, a 'still small voice' coming from within the brain says in effect, 'You're unhappy— why not put an end to it all—don't think you're anything special either as a soul, a physical organism, a special creation of God, or anything else—and don't think that there's any particular purpose or good working itself out through all this suffering in the universe, for there isn't'. That is to give a summary in more or less modern terms of the attitude presented by one of the 'voices'. The other voice finds answers. At first it is hard-going but eventually the balance of argument turns in his favour; the 'gloomy' voice finds it harder to think of replies and ultimately, as daylight comes, it sullenly withdraws from the fray.

The Two Voices is one of Tennyson's most impressive poems. The arguments are vigorously and memorably expressed on both sides. The three-line verses (one hundred and fifty of them) are wonderfully sustained, each group of lines bunched like a little knot of thought to be attacked by the idea which is its negation. And, although the last section has often been criticised, I do not myself find it as inadequate or sentimental as is generally suggested. The thinker, the 'I' of the poem, looks out from his window, reflects, cynically at first (for it is the 'bad' voice that first makes the observation), that this is Sunday morning; hears the bells, and watches the people going, presumably, to eight o'clock communion. Then come the verses that are usually cited for derision:

> One walk'd between his wife and child,
> With measured footfall firm and mild,
> And now and then he gravely smiled.
>
> The prudent partner of his blood
> Lean'd on him, faithful, gentle, good,
> Wearing the rose of womanhood.
>
> And in their double love secure,
> The little maiden walk'd demure,
> Pacing with downward eyelids pure.
>
> These three made unity so sweet,
> My frozen heart began to beat,
> Remembering its ancient heat.

There is something comical about them, it is true: that gravely smiling father, the mother who leans on him, and their pure, demure little daughter. In fact the 'bad' voice begins to protest within the reader. 'Pious prigs!' it says. 'The old man probably commits a hundred crimes a week in the name of business. He probably pays his employees starvation wages; the old girl is probably narrow-minded and a terror to the housemaids; and the little one will soon become a spoilt coquette, with those downward-turned eyelids of hers'. Maybe so; Tennyson has unwittingly called cynicism into play by making his family so very, and so Victorianly, perfect. But the cynical commentary is not necessarily the true one and in any case it misses the point. That is, that as one emerges from a depressed state one looks about at the world with a heart newly moved by familiar things. The church-goers are (were) a common enough sight, but now, under the emotional stress of a night that has brought the thinker to the verge of suicide, he looks at them afresh, is moved even to 'bless' them (as the Ancient Mariner finds himself blessing the water-snakes), and a new hope takes charge of his heart. The three people stand in his mind for goodness in mankind, and more specifically for the goodness which is promoted in society around him by a well-ordered family life. The 'bad' voice may have things to say about that too. But it cannot argue such goodness out of existence, and in the emotional condition which the poem records, the knowledge of such goodness is sufficient to confirm a new hope that has come in the place of despair:

> I wonder'd, while I paced along:
> The woods were fill'd so full with song,
> There seem'd no room for sense of wrong;
>
> And all so variously wrought,
> I marvell'd how the mind was brought
> To anchor by one gloomy thought;
>
> And wherefore rather I made choice
> To commune with that barren voice,
> Than him that said, 'Rejoice! Rejoice!'

There is, I think, a valid criticism of *The Two Voices*. An American writer, J. H. Buckley, says of its argument that it 'moves by delays towards its preconceived solution'. In other words, although the counter-arguments of the 'bad' voice are fully expressed in the various stages of the poem, Tennyson really knew from the start that he was going to make the 'good' voice triumph, and you can see him manipulating the arguments to that end; the poem, then, is a consciously thought-out piece of dialectic; one does not feel that the material took charge of the imagination, rather that the determination to come to an optimistic conclusion took charge of the writer. *The Two Voices*, in fact, has somewhat the same relationship to *The Lotos-Eaters* as *The Palace of Art* has to *The Lady of Shalott*. *The Two Voices* and *The Palace of Art* both argue a case, using imaginative poetic means to do it. *The Lotos-Eaters* and *The Lady of Shalott* are creations of a different kind. Here the imagination is in charge, and the conscious mind (arguing things out in verse) is in abeyance or is all taken up in the business of creating. But these two poems, by the richness of suggestion that is in them, offer more to the mind than do the consciously 'intellectual' pair. And they are ultimately, I think, more genuine

Tennyson. Oscar Wilde said 'Give a man a mask and he will tell you the truth'. In *The Lotos-Eaters* Tennyson has the mask of Ulysses' sailors: he can quite justly say, 'This is not me talking; it is these men'. In *The Lady of Shalott* he has the mask of the story-teller: he can truthfully say, 'I am not moralising, I am telling you a story'. But in *The Palace of Art* and *The Two Voices* he is Alfred Tennyson standing naked before the nineteenth-century public. In both poems he exposes his own spiritual dilemma with wonderful frankness, but in both his solution is the one which the public wanted of him. He was not being hypocritical in arriving at these conclusions: they were the answers he thought to be right. But deeper in him were feelings beyond the grip of the consciously arguing mind, and we are closest to these in the poems where the creative imagination is most in control.

There is, then, much unintentional or unconscious self-revelation in Tennyson's work, and it can take rather more subtle forms than those already discussed. The poem called *Supposed Confessions of a Second-rate Sensitive Mind* is a case in point. It was written during the Cambridge period, published in 1830, and is one of the first examples in English literature of the dramatic monologue. A character is imagined, made to speak in the first person, and we learn about him and his feelings as the piece proceeds. In this way the poet himself is masked, and so the 'Confessions' must not, on the face of it, be regarded as Tennyson's own, but as those of his creation, a man with 'a sensitive, second-rate mind'. This character, we gather, is in a wretched condition, a mood of extreme depression rather like that in which *The Two Voices* begins. He appears to have lost his faith, his energy and his hope. He was brought up in a Christian household but, with the intellectual drive and pride of adolescence, he wanted to test the truth of traditional beliefs, to sift evidence, construct his own creed after a study of all religions, and to reject whatever seemed false. Now he regrets this. He knows, from seeing it in other people, what a sense of security the Christian faith can bring; he knows that he has lost this and yearns to retrieve it.

Now it might be assumed, following the discussion of *The Lady of Shalott* and *The Lotos-Eaters*, that what we have here is really the confessions of Alfred Tennyson; that once more safely behind the mask, he can express his own doubts and in fact reveal his own loss of faith. The truth is not so simple. The poem does suggest a great deal about its author, but one of its features is that, though the character thinks himself to be without faith, his belief in God is not really in question at all. The monologue begins and ends as a prayer: it is specifically addressed to God without any sort of qualification such as 'if any God there be'. The confidence that there exists a supernatural being who has a special relationship with man is complete. So what the poem tells us about the masked poet is not that he was a secret disbeliever, but that his belief in God was so fundamental to him that when he tried to enter the mind of a man without belief he could not do it.

On the other hand, the morbid state of the 'second-rate mind' had much in common with Tennyson's own condition. 'My gloomed fancy', he refers to, and this sounds very like Tennyson brooding over the black-blood of his family and his own share of it. 'O weary life!' he exclaims, using that most Tennysonian of adjectives. There is also, in the *Supposed Confessions*, the nostalgia and the wish to evade the responsibilities of adult independence and to escape back into the world of childhood:

> Thrice happy state again to be
> The trustful infant on the knee!
> Who lets his rosy fingers play
> About his mother's neck, and knows
> Nothing beyond his mother's eyes.

Of course it is the second-rate character talking and not Tennyson, but taking it with all the other poems which concern a yearning for escape in some form, one cannot help but see something of the creator's character in it also.

It was many years before Tennyson publicly expressed his or anybody else's 'gloomed fancies' with as little to lighten the darkness as in the *Supposed Confessions*. In *The Two Voices* the 'good' voice is made to out-argue the 'bad': belief in life and purpose triumph over pessimism and depression. Even *In Memoriam* asserts hope and represents a victory over death and despair. Not until *Maud* (1856) did he again express a neurotic, black mind, without providing a counterbalancing hopefulness readily acceptable to his readers. And in a whole series of poems, the 1842 volume presents subjects that deal in strength, goodness and belief in progress.

One poem that would normally have appeared with the others in 1842 was interestingly suppressed. *Tithonus*, written in 1833, was not published till 1860, presumably because its mood and outlook checked the more optimistic spirit which Tennyson wanted the 1842 volume to embody. The myth of Tithonus tells how as a youth he was carried off from Troy by the goddess Eos on account of his beauty. She obtained for him the gift of immortality, but forgot to ask Zeus for eternal youth as well. In Tennyson's poem the infinitely aged immortal speaks, weary and yearning for death as a release. In spite of its subject this is not one of the 'dark poems'. The old man does not speak cynically about life; he is not bitter or gloomy about anything other than his own 'cruel immortality'. On the contrary, he envies 'the kindly race of men' and there still lives in him an aching sense of beauty—of earth and sky, of Eos and of himself in former times. The poem is one of the most beautiful Tennyson wrote. What does seem significant and characteristic is that the best poetry should again be drawn from him by just such a subject. For Tithonus, though existing in perfect stillness, remote as the lotos-eaters from the turmoil of ordinary life, has no will, no energy. His condition makes it possible for the poet to recapture that Keatsian mood, 'half in love with easeful death', which had inspired him to write his best poetry in *Mariana*. He never wrote better than in the first lines of *Tithonus*:

> The woods decay, the woods decay and fall,
> The vapours weep their burthen to the ground,
> Man comes and tills the field and lies beneath,
> And after many a summer dies the swan.

Sound and image combine to enforce sense: to represent age and the sorrows of age, natural law and the beneficence of it. The heavy, regular beat of

> Man comes and tills the field and lies beneath

emphasises the kindly security that the natural rhythm of existence brings to the normal man. Aldous Huxley (in *Texts and Pretexts*) asks what the swan is doing in the picture and calls it a 'luminous irrelevance'. F. L. Lucas has answered that it is not: it is a symbol of age, and whiteness too reflects the 'white-hair'd shadow' that the old man now is, sitting:

> Here at the quiet limit of the world.

In either case, as Huxley says, 'Tennyson knew his magician's business'.

It might be added that (instinctively) he knew his publisher's business, too. Press and public alike found the 1842 volume largely to their taste. Among the virtues commended was the more 'wholesome' tone of the poems, the emergence (as one review put it) from 'the twilight fantasies of his earlier poems to the broad daylight of sound feeling and pure taste'. He was beginning, they thought, to show qualities which would inspire his generation with further hope and faith in human progress. There was discernible a new strength and a firmer moral purpose. Into this account *Tithonus* could be fitted only with difficulty, while its companion-piece, *Ulysses*, fitted very well indeed. And this, of course, Tennyson published.

Both poems are dramatic monologues based on classical legend and spoken by old men. In other respects they are antithetical. Tithonus longs for death; Ulysses craves 'life piled on life'. Where Ulysses is active ('Old age hath yet his honour and his toil . . . some work of noble note may yet be done'), Tithonus decays, will-less, a 'gray shadow, once a man'. For Ulysses, a new world opens up as he looks about him to the horizon:

> my purpose holds
> To sail beyond the sunset, and the baths
> Of all the western stars.

But for Tithonus, the heavens, 'the gleaming halls of morn', bring only the painful renewal of an existence that is no life. This very existence too is dreamlike, a merely glimmering consciousness, still agonisingly sensitive to the beauty of nature, yet using even this beauty as a sort of anaesthetic to drug the conscious mind into that trance-like condition where reality is bearable. Ulysses is sharp and precise:

> There lies the port; the vessel puffs her sail.

Above all, where *Tithonus* enervates, *Ulysses* braces. It does so, moreover, with the command of rhetoric that a hundred years later was to be known as Churchillian:

> One equal temper of heroic hearts,
> Made weak by time and fate, but strong in will
> To strive, to seek, to find, and not to yield.

Tithonus can do nothing to compete with this sort of thing.

Perhaps on re-reading, however, one might have some second thoughts about *Ulysses*. The words are so stirring, the scene is so colourful and the spirit so manly that one can overlook the fact that this too is really a poem of escape. Look at it with an unenchanted eye and what one sees is an old man abandoning his old wife, his responsibilities, the people under his rule, the slow labour of bringing them 'through soft degrees . . . to the useful and the good', and leaving his son behind to get on with it. He calls himself 'an idle king' with a kind of contempt for the unexciting arts of peaceful government. He also speaks in the grandiose terms of the egotist: 'I cannot rest from travel; I will drink life to the lees'. And off he goes on some hare-brained scheme to 'touch the Happy Isles'. This, of course, is an irreverent commentary, one which is being deliberately 'awkward'. Tennyson presents an adventurous, aspiring and exceptional leader, and the dignity of language befits the nobility of soul. But the facts remain that there is another way of looking at the situation and that Tennyson does not see it. He has presented us with that insidious kind of escapism which renounces sober responsibility in favour of excitement; and he does not even see that it is a form of escapism. This is the kind of thing W. H. Auden has in mind when he asks: 'What is *Ulysses* but a covert . . . refusal to be a responsible and useful person and a glorification of the heroical dandy?' But to Tennyson and his contemporaries it was very uplifting, bracing the spirit to live greatly, look to the future and keep cheerful in old age, for:

> Tho' much is taken, much abides.

The future also looms large in *Locksley Hall*. Ulysses sails westward and the reader's mind turns to the unknown lands that were awaiting an adventurous spirit there. The speaker of *Locksley Hall*, the 'I' of the poem, also thinks to set himself free from the limitations of his present life:

> . . . to burst all links of habit—there to wander far away,
> On from island unto island at the gateways of the day.

Along with his own future, he speculates about the world's; and this brings the famous verses of prophecy:

> For I dipt into the future, far as human eye could see,
> Saw the Vision of the world, and all the wonder that would be;
>
> Saw the heavens fill with commerce, argosies of magic sails,
> Pilots of the purple twilight, dropping down with costly bales;
>
> Heard the heavens fill with shouting, and there rain'd a ghastly dew
> From the nations' airy navies grappling in the central blue;
>
> Far along the world-wide whisper of the south-wind rushing warm,
> With the standards of the peoples plunging thro' the thunderstorm;
>
> Till the war-drum throbb'd no longer, and the battle-flags were furl'd
> In the Parliament of man, the Federation of the world.

The lines seem to foretell in a rather marvellous way the coming of the aeroplane, of aerial warfare and of world war, the League of Nations and U.N.O. itself. With it goes a faith that ultimately all will be well:

> There the common sense of most shall hold a fretful realm in awe,
> And the kindly earth shall slumber, lapt in universal law.

The Future and Progress are equated:

> Not in vain the distance beacons. Forward, forward let us range,
> Let the great world spin for ever down the ringing grooves of change.

> Thro' the shadow of the globe we sweep into the younger day:
> Better fifty years of Europe than a cycle of Cathay.

The lines ring and swing: they are firm, epigrammatic and memorable. They are a kind of *locus classicus*: what very oft was thought in Victorian England but ne'er so quotably expressed.

Yet they are spoken by a desperately unstable character in a poem where again two voices are audible. One of the voices is heavy with scepticism, the voice of 'the palsied heart . . . the jaundiced eye':

> Eye, to which all order festers, all things here are out of joint:
> Science moves, but slowly, slowly, creeping on from point to point.

Perhaps, moreover, the progress of science will not bring happiness, any more than knowledge inevitably brings wisdom; and, for himself, the speaker feels that happiness might even involve a reversal of progress, with its machinery and its literature, its inhibitions and frustrations:

> There methinks would be enjoyment more than in this march of mind
> In the steamship, in the railway, in the thoughts that shake mankind.

> There the passions cramp'd no longer shall have scope and breathing space;

I will take some savage woman, she shall rear my dusky race.

Iron-jointed, supple-sinew'd, they shall dive and they shall run,
Catch the wild goat by the hair, and hurl their lances in the sun;

Whistle back the parrot's call, and leap the rainbows of the brooks,
Not with blinded eyesight poring over miserable books—

Here the 'dark' voice breaks off, and the other half of this strangely divided mind takes over: 'Fools, again the dream, the fancy! but I *know* my words are wild'. The dark side of the speaker's mind, desperate at having loved and lost, at finding himself also the victim of a money-ridden society, is very like the spirit that Tennyson was to dramatise and explore more fully in *Maud*. It is also far closer than is the 'reasonable' and cheerful voice to the tone of *Locksley Hall Sixty Years After*, in which Tennyson at eighty, fiercely formidable and sternly authoritative, cast a bleak eye to the future as he saw it at that time:

'Forward' rang the voices then, and of the many mine was one,
Let us hush this cry of 'Forward' till ten thousand years have gone.

Change, he had found, was not necessarily progress. It had brought more than its share of horrors in his own lifetime, and, he feared, was to bring more. But in 1841, when *Locksley Hall* was written, 'the march of mind' meant Progress, and Progress should be encouraged.

'Balance' is a key-term in the discussion of all these poems. All involve a division of the mind. In *The Palace of Art*, *The Two Voices* and *Locksley Hall*, the debate is open and explicit. In *Tithonus* is expressed a way of thought and feeling that is contrasted with its companion-piece *Ulysses*. The *Supposed Confessions* develops a line of argument which we are supposed to see (the speaker himself does so) as wrong. *Mariana* and *The Lotos-Eaters* present states of feeling, conditions of life, upon which no explicit judgement is made, yet which we know concerned intimately the debating mind of the poet himself. *The Lady of Shalott* is a tale in which many of these issues find a symbol or with which they at any rate strike a resonance. In one other poem, debate and choice again figure prominently, and it too binds many Tennysonian strands together. This is *Oenone*, a lyrical monologue spoken by the girl whom Prince Paris of Troy had taken as his bride and deserted when he carried off Helen. She tells how Paris won her and how the three goddesses came to him offering him a choice of gifts.

Paris, of course, should have chosen wisdom. He was offered it by Pallas but chose Aphrodite's gift of love. The other gift, offered by Hera and also renounced, was power. Tennyson's way of presenting this temptation is interesting:

> men, in power
> Only, are likest gods, who have attain'd
> Rest in a happy place and quiet seats
> Above the thunder, with undying bliss
> In knowledge of their own supremacy.

It is not the glory, the excitement, the opportunity or the responsibility of power which is stressed, but its most passive attribute: security. Security, moreover, is valued not because it makes possible good works or anything active at all; it is rather that security is a necessary condition of repose. Kings are like gods are like lotos-eaters: it is a very Tennysonian kind of temptation. Love, the gift of Aphrodite, is presented as the temptation of sensuality. Paris falls for this and thus sets in motion the events which are to lead to the great war and the fall of Troy, all beginning with his seizure of the beautiful Helen. We are reminded of these tragic consequences in the last lines of the poem. The Trojan war has not yet begun, but these lines carry intimations of the disaster to come:

> I will rise and go
> Down into Troy, and ere the stars come forth
> Talk with the wild Cassandra, for she says
> A fire dances before her, and a sound
> Rings ever in her ears of armed men.
> What this may be I know not, but I know
> That whereso'er I am by night and day,
> All earth and air seem only burning fire.

The last two lines are the poet's way of linking the future and the past. For Paris has already brought tragedy; or rather, the indulgence of sensuality has brought it. Oenone loved Paris for his good looks: she makes it clear that the first sight of him inflamed her passions and so their union was based on sexual attraction. With Oenone this grew into love, but Paris left her, and so, as it seems to the Victorian moralist, she pays for her indulgence. The fire of passion becomes now a burning torment of bitterness and loss, just as the passion that led Helen to leave her husband and follow Paris will start a fire big enough to consume whole civilisations. In the face of this, we are left to ponder the wisdom of Pallas, who offers:

> Self-reverence, self-knowledge, self-control.

'Right is right' and so 'to follow right' fearless of consequence is true wisdom.

Out of all the conflicting voices in Tennyson's poetry throughout this period, then, there emerges the clear voice of Pallas Athene. The tone is somewhat cold, as is the picture of the goddess herself (her spear is 'cold', her breast is 'snow-cold', and her eye is 'full and earnest'). The doctrine is also somewhat at odds with the hazy, languid and sensuous beauty of the poem. It enunciates principles opposed on the one hand to a life of mere security and on the other to the indulgence of sensuality. They are definite and uncompromising. For better or worse, Tennyson tried hard, and with much success, to live and work by them to the end of his days.

5

Hallam's Death: Tennyson's Marriage

'. . . carrying a bit of Chaos . . . which he is manufacturing
into Cosmos' (Thomas Carlyle)

Of the poems just discussed, the *Supposed Confessions* and
Mariana belong to the volume of 1830, *The Lady of Shalott*,
The Lotos-Eaters and *The Palace of Art* and *Oenone* to 1832,
Ulysses, *Locksley Hall* and *The Two Voices* to 1842 (*Tithonus*,
as explained, though written in 1833 was not published till
1860). These alone would have been sufficient to have made
young Tennyson a name much talked about in his own age and
for a long time after. But the volumes contain twice as many
famous and admired poems: the *Ode to Memory* and *The
Kraken* in 1830; *Mariana in the South*, *The Miller's Daughter*
and *The May-Queen* in 1832; *Morte d'Arthur*, *Dora*, *The Vision
of Sin*, *St. Simeon Stylites* and *Lady Clara* in 1842. Many conflicting statements have been made about the reception of these
publications, for as well as a great deal of praise there was
adverse criticism, some of it fierce. There is no question, however, that by 1842 he was among the living poets most read and
most discussed, and by 1850 he was Poet Laureate.

Tennyson himself held that his essential biography was in his
poems; through the poems we come to know him, through
biography we only observe. It is also clear that as he got older
so his life became more settled and, to the observer, less interesting. The 'thirties and 'forties, however, were still years in which
things were happening to him, fundamental events in any man's
experience: his father died, his best friend died, he made his
name and lost his money, he fell in love and was loved in return.

The years were full of contrast: of great emotional stress and also of varied, easy-going travel. When the period came to an end, it was in great good fortune, for the same wonderful year brought the publication of *In Memoriam*, the appointment as Poet Laureate, and marriage to Emily Sellwood after a virtual engagement of fourteen years. Tennyson had then lived exactly half his life, and the century was exactly half-way through.

His fame certainly began in Cambridge. His friends, the Apostles, were sure of his genius, were not backward in expressing opinions, and were not without influence both through their families and through their own abilities and subsequent careers. Some of them were still writing reviews of Tennyson's publications long after he and they had become well-established in the world. The inner circle of enthusiasts sent out 'advance information' in all directions. One, who was to become the Dean of Ely, wrote to his father, 'I have got the third of the Tennysons in my room, who is an immense poet', and Arthur Hallam wrote to Gladstone that he believed Tennyson might well be the greatest poet of the century. After the publication of *Timbuctoo* in 1829 Charles Wordsworth (afterwards a Bishop) wrote to his brother Christopher: 'if it had come out with Lord Byron's name, it would have been thought as fine as anything he ever wrote'. Another Christopher Wordsworth, their father, was then Master of Trinity and he was perhaps the best-connected of all, for his brother William occasionally visited him. In 1830 the great poet was able to report of the literary scene at Cambridge: 'we have a respectable show of blossom in poetry. Two brothers of the name of Tennyson in particular are not a little promising'.

At least such praise as this helped to sweeten the conditions under which Tennyson went down from the University. His father died in March, 1831, and Tennyson did not return to take his degree. He was at this time worried about his eyesight. 'Alfred is trying to make his eyes bad enough to require an aegrotat degree', wrote his friend Merivale. But the distress was genuine even if the complaint was exaggerated. It was all part of a theory of compensation: because his hearing was abnormally acute, because he was abnormally near-sighted, and because he was a poet—like Milton and Homer—he thought he might well be doomed to blindness. This anxiety seems to have been allayed by the summer, but some new problems arose to take its place. The family began more and more to depend on him as Edward and Septimus became more wretched and incapable. There was the problem of 'finding something for Arthur' and then for Horatio, the youngest brother. There were also formidable debts accruing: Dr. Tennyson owed £882 when he died, Frederick left Cambridge owing £330, Charles £320, and even Alfred had managed to raise a bill of £172. These, admittedly, presented no problem in Somersby, for nothing could be done about them. They were duly passed on to old grandfather Tennyson who grimly settled them.

The troubles of these years were mitigated above all by the friendship of Arthur Hallam. In the summer of 1830 Hallam and Tennyson had been away together on the abortive enterprise to the Pyrenees. In 1832 they went to the Rhine on what was probably the happiest holiday of Tennyson's life. In the meantime during one of his visits to Somersby, Hallam had won the heart and, he hoped, the hand of Tennyson's sister Emily. In 1833 he came again to Somersby, and again life seems to have been wonderfully full and happy for all of them. Later in the year, Hallam undertook a tour of Europe with his father, and on the fifteenth of September he died. Very slightly feverish, he had lain down on the couch in his room at Vienna, while his father went out for a walk. On his return Mr. Hallam thought Arthur was asleep and wrote some letters. But there had been a haemorrhage of the brain, and the greatly loved young man was no more.

Alfred had lost his friend, Emily her lover. She was ill for the best part of a year and at times it seemed she would die: 'if I die (which the Tennysons never do) . . .' was a grim clause in one of her letters. The record of Tennyson's grief is *In Memoriam*. The poem was not published till seventeen years after Hallam's death, but the writing of it began almost immediately. One of Tennyson's 1833 notebooks contains five sections of the poem, and in between two of them comes the first draft of

Morte d'Arthur. Grief takes many forms: with Tennyson it seems to have given an excess of energy, an intellectual and emotional stirring, calling up the creative powers to more abundant life. *Ulysses* was written very shortly after Hallam died, and Tennyson said it 'gave my feeling about the need of going forward, and braving the struggle of life perhaps more simply than anything in *In Memoriam*'. *The Two Voices*, originally called *Thoughts of a Suicide*, also dates from that time; so do perhaps half a dozen other published poems. One of his friends, R. J. Tennant, writes: 'Alfred although much broken in spirits is yet able to divert his thoughts from gloomy brooding, and keep his mind in activity'. He planned his studies carefully, conscious of a narrowness of education and of a poet's need to have a wide intellectual range. Perhaps there is something schoolboyish in the time-table he drew up; I do not know how long he stuck to it.

Monday.	History, German.
Tuesday.	Chemistry, German.
Wednesday.	Botany, German.
Thursday.	Electricity, German.
Friday.	Animal Physiology, German.
Saturday.	Mechanics.
Sunday.	Theology.
Next Week.	Italian in the afternoon.
Third Week.	Greek. Evenings. Poetry.

Family duties must have taken up much of his energy. Old grandfather Tennyson died in 1835 and the next year brought all the stresses of closing down the home and leaving Somersby. For four years the Tennysons lived happily at Epping Forest, then for a short time at Boxley near Maidstone, and after this at 10, St. James's Square, Cheltenham. There were other disturbances. Tennyson had met Emily Sellwood in 1830, had asked her in the woods near Somersby whether she was a Dryad or an Oread, and seems to have thought no more about her till she turned up as a bridesmaid at his brother Charles's wedding in 1836. He then wrote a poem about her (*The Bridesmaid*), pretty and passionless, one would have thought—a little auto-graph-album poem. Anyway, he fell in love and the love lasted a lifetime. It survived family opposition (the Sellwoods were not keen on the penniless poet), and it emerged triumphant at a quiet wedding in 1850.

Not that the poet was consistently penniless during this time. From land and by legacy he had in 1840 a fortune of £3,000. Unfortunately he soon found a way of losing it. While at Boxley, the family had met Matthew Allen, a doctor in charge of the lunatic asylum at Fairmead. He seems to have been a good doctor, a philanthropic and imaginative human being ('a specu-lative, hopeful, earnest-frothy man' was Carlyle's description), but very bad or unlucky at business. He wanted to float an enterprise to promote wood-carving by machinery. This was thought to be sound commercially and beneficial socially, and Dr. Allen persuaded Tennyson to put his £3,000 into it. It went badly from the start. The first models sent out from Birmingham came apart in transit ('Let Brummagem look to it,' wrote Tennyson, 'or she will ruin her reputation'). Brother Frederick might possibly have saved the situation for he was the wealthiest of the family, but though repeatedly importuned by Dr. Allen, Frederick had other things to do with his money. By 1843 all had failed and, though Brummagem was not ruined, Dr. Allen and the Tennysons were. Friends rallied round. One of them took out a life insurance policy in the name of Dr. Allen who more or less promptly died. Tennyson recovered much of what he had lost, but the circumstances saddened his good fortune: 'No gladness crossed my heart, but sorrow and pity', he wrote. 'That's not theatrical but the truth.' This was in 1845 and in the meantime, marriage now out of the question, Tennyson had sunk desperately low in spirits and in health. 'What with ruin in the distance and hypochondriacs in the foreground, God help us all.'

Perhaps He did, for Sir Robert Peel, the Prime Minister, who had read *Ulysses* with approval and had been in touch with Henry Hallam, Arthur's father, came to the rescue with a State pension. Alfred was now guaranteed £200 a year. One of the Apostles 'had a sense of the ludicrous' in the 'snug' annuity, but its recipient had only thankfulness. With it came a certain freedom. The family was no longer in such distress and Tennyson could travel. Not that he had been relentlessly tied to home in the intervening years, but his travels had been confined to this country: the South Coast in 1835, the Lake District in 1836, then down to Torquay. In Wales he marvelled how fluently the little boys and girls spoke Welsh; in Stratford he thought the Shakespeare monument a poor thing but wrote his name on the wall of the birthplace. These were what Auden calls Tennyson's 'tavern years'. He took 'lonely walks in dark valleys' and then called in for his pint of port (there was always something huge about the man—even his tea he took in a bowl, calling an ordinary cupful 'a niggardly allowance'). On one of these occasions he wrote a short poem to 'Mine Host':

Yon huddled cloud his motion shifts,
    Where, by the tavern in the dale,
The thirsty horseman, nodding, lifts
    The creaming horn of corny ale!

This tavern is his chief resort,
    For he, whose cellar is his pride,
Gives stouter ale and riper port
    Than any in the country-side.

Mine host is fat, and gray, and wise,
    He strokes his beard before he speaks;
And when he laughs, his little eyes
    Are swallow'd in his pamper'd cheeks.

He brims his beaker to the top,
    With jokes you never heard before,
And sometimes with a twinkling drop,
    'To those who will not taste it more!'

This was found by Hallam Tennyson in one of his father's notebooks. When he published it in the *Memoir* he substituted 'his' in the second verse for 'our', which is what Alfred had less guardedly written.

The 'tavern years' were also the 'silent years'. After the volume that appeared at the very end of 1832, Tennyson published nothing apart from two short poems till 1842. The reason was not his grief at Hallam's death as was sometimes thought. It was far more an extreme reluctance to expose himself again to criticism. Everyone who knew him found it remarkable that he could, even late in life, be so upset by a hostile phrase. 'All the mass of eulogy he took comparatively little notice of, but he could never forget an unfriendly word, even from the most obscure, insignificant and unknown quarter.' So wrote Sir James Knowles, the architect of Tennyson's last home, Aldworth. 'He knew it was a weakness in him, and could be laughed out of it for a time, but it soon returned upon him and had given him from his earliest youth exaggerated vexation.' The early volumes recei ed much praise, but also enough abuse to make such a man dread a repetition. After all the praise meted out to the 1830 volume, Christopher North (a pseudonym) had written in *Blackwood's Magazine*: 'Alfred is as an owl: all that he wants is to be shot, stuffed and stuck into a glass case, to be made immortal in a museum' (this was apropos a poem called *The Owl*, and certainly one of the more regrettable pieces). The writer also admitted at the end of his article that he had been rather crabby and that Alfred Tennyson was undoubtedly a poet. But the '1833' volume brought criticism that was much more general. All except one of the reviews spoke of high promise, ability and achievement, but there were repeated complaints that the poetry was wild and unintelligible, that there were serious metrical defects and an unwholesomeness in the art which did not offer a strong moral content as well as mere beauty. The most vicious attack came from the most influential literary journal of the day, the *Quarterly*. Several writers, including J. S. Mill, came to Tennyson's defence, and the damage to his reputation was probably not so very severe in the long run. But it worried Tennyson to distraction. He even thought of emigrating, and to his friend James Spedding he wrote: 'I do not wish to be dragged forward again in any shape before the reading public at present'. That was in 1835. When he did publish again, in 1842, some of the earlier poems had been suppressed by him, many had been changed (generally for the better), and of the thirty-six new poems all were written in metres that were standard and well-known. He was duly rewarded. The literary journals were complimentary. The *Edinburgh Review* found 'the interest deeper and purer—there is more humanity with less image and drapery'. *Blackwood's* now saw 'the indisputable impress of genius, bearing throughout the spirit of religion'. And even the *Quarterly* changed its tone. But then, by that time, an ex-Apostle had the reviewing to do, and John Wilson Croker, the writer of the earlier attack, was furious but powerless.

But although the 1842 volume triumphed, and although Tennyson's reputation grew markedly during the following years, there was still a good deal of criticism, and particularly a pressure upon him to write 'responsibly'. This meant that he was to *teach* more.

> He has no excuse, therefore, for expending his precious hours, his glowing thoughts, and his sweet-toned voice, in painting the hues of the peacock's tail. . . . We have had enough of the past; we have had enough of description, and passion, and cold reflection; we now want sympathy, and hope, and direction. Alfred Tennyson was born and lives at a time when men are shouting in the wilderness of the world, 'Oh, for a better time!!' He might have been the herald of a new era; the prophet-preacher of a 'good time coming'. . . . But he wanted courage to become a teacher, and left to far less capable men the direction of the mind of the masses. . . . Why does not Alfred Tennyson leave the Midian of his retirement to point the people's way to the coming Canaan?

Thus *Hogg's Weekly Instructor* on Christmas Day 1847. *Locksley Hall*, evidently, was not enough. Nor was *The Princess*.

Yet *The Princess*, published in November, 1847, was among other things a deliberate attempt to meet such criticisms as this. 'Seldom has a poem owed so much to contemporary literary doctrine,' writes E. F. Shannon in a superbly documented book called *Tennyson and the Reviewers* (1952). One of the doctrines held that poetry must contribute to the solution of social problems (it is odd to find the Marxist view of literature so closely anticipated by Victorian orthodoxy). So in *The Princess* Tennyson takes up the subject of education for women. 'Let him ascertain his mission and work his work,' urged a helpful critic in 1840. In women's rights he found a mission, and he duly got down to the work. Another writer had felt that Tennyson would now 'find himself able to fly a higher flight than lyric, idyll, or eclogue, and we counsel him to try it'. In other words, a *long* poem was required, and over three thousand words were accordingly produced. Moreover, critics and public alike looked for warm feeling and wholesome good humour, and they could here find the first in the second half of the poem, the second in the first. They also liked to hear about progress, 'the golden future time', and Tennyson also met this wish, with lines like these, from the Conclusion:

> This fine old world of ours is but a child
> Yet in the go-cart. Patience! Give it time
> To learn its limbs: there is a hand that guides.

But all the recommendations of press and public, dutifully observed and sincerely applied, did not make *The Princess* a great poem, and Tennyson knew it. 'My book is out', he wrote to Fitzgerald, 'and I hate it, and so no doubt will you', adding: 'Never mind, you will like me none the worse, and now goodnight. I am knocked up, and going to bed'. He revised it again and again, but his own lines in the Conclusion of the poem stand as a wry confession of failure:

> Then rose a little feud betwixt the two,
> Betwixt the mockers and the realists:
> And I, betwixt them both, to please them both,
> And yet to give the story as it rose,
> I moved as in a strange diagonal,
> And maybe neither pleased myself nor them.

It is a very strange poem indeed. Partly a burlesque (its story provided the basis of the Gilbert and Sullivan opera, *Princess*

Ida), it tells a tale of knights and ladies, quite deliberately fantastic and mock-serious for much of the time. Ida, the daughter of King Gama, has founded a university for women. No man is allowed to enter the bounds, and Ida herself has renounced mankind, including the Prince to whom she was promised in infancy by parental agreement. This Prince, who tells the tale, has other ideas. He already loves her picture and expects to love her. His father, impatient of all such tomfoolery, tells King Gama that he must deliver his daughter as promised or there will be war. But in the meantime the Prince, with two of his friends, has gone to look for himself and, disguised as women, the young men enter the University. So much for the comic-opera element. There is also the 'theme': the place, character and education of women. The story-telling is set in modern times. The Prologue introduces us to a group of friends, seven of them, who are chatting with some ladies. The day has been that one in the year on which Sir Walter Vivian opens his stately home to the public. The crowd (the holiday of a Mechanics Institute had given Tennyson the idea) is happy, the day 'genial', and the conversation turns on an old story about a warrior princess. To entertain the ladies, the young men make up a story, its subject suggested by this old tale. Each of them is to contribute a chapter of his own, following on where the last narrator left off (Tennyson and his Apostle friends used to do this sometimes at Cambridge). There are seven sections; hence the sub-title *A Medley*. We return to the present for the conclusion, so the piece is set within a modern framework, and though the question of women's rights is not discussed directly, it is clear that the old tale is meant to focus upon it as a modern problem.

Tennyson was not the first to bring the question before the public. Mary Wollstonecraft's *Vindication of the Rights of Women* came out in 1792 and this was the pioneer work. Since then two influential papers, the *Edinburgh* and *Westminster Reviews*, had repeatedly supported the cause. E. F. Shannon points out that one of the reviews of Tennyson's own poems had stressed the importance of the educated woman and had at the same time urged the poet towards sustained enthusiasm for a particular cause. Even so, Tennyson was among the advanced men of his time in showing active concern and a large measure of sympathy.

Not that his treatment was of a kind likely to arouse any very revolutionary feeling in others. His attitude was not that of the out-and-out advocate: one sometimes wonders indeed whether it comes to much more than King Gama's admission, 'There is something in it'. Apparently many of his readers thought that Tennyson's presentation of the women's university was meant as satire, and although he made alterations designed to prevent that misconception, one can still see how it arose. Perhaps the most telling passages as propaganda are the ones where the Prince's father voices the conventional, rough-and-ready, no-nonsense view of those who do *not* think that 'there is something in it', as in these lines from Part 5:

> Man for the field and woman for the hearth:
> Man for the sword and for the needle she:
> Man with the head and woman with the heart:
> Man to command and woman to obey.

It is pleasant to see Tennyson as satirist. The King shows such coarseness of intellect throughout the tale that his attitude to the character and relation of the sexes is easily seen to be barbaric and inadequate: in other words, a social theory is satirised through the very person of its advocate. Still, Ida's isolated university life will not satisfy, and a compromise is eventually reached in which the Prince takes Ida to wife (that involves the domesticity which she has renounced), nevertheless esteeming her as an intelligent, an equal being, 'to live and learn and be All that harms not distinctive womanhood' (Part 7). 'Henceforth', he tells her:

> thou hast a helper, me, that know
> The woman's cause is man's: they rise or sink
> Together, dwarf'd or godlike, bond or free.

Much more could be said about *The Princess* that is beyond the scope of this study. The poem is odd, interesting, and ultimately impressive in several other respects. Not least, perhaps, in that one comes to find interest and enjoyment in a piece that at first may seem an utter waste of time. Recollections of my own first readings are principally of impatience at a silly tale, a half-hearted and inappropriate treatment, a rather flat, undistinguished style, suddenly relieved by lyrics like 'Now sleeps the crimson petal', 'Sweet and Low' and 'Come down, O Maid', which would do far better on their own. I think more kindly of it now; and not least, I must add, because of the valuable critical lights provided by Valerie Pitt in her book *Tennyson Laureate* (pp. 140-147).

Carlyle said of Tennyson at about this period that he struck him as 'a man . . . carrying a bit of Chaos about him, in short, which he is manufacturing into Cosmos'. In *The Princess* one can see the process at work. Some Chaos remains. The comic and the serious elements in the poem do not get on well together (Tennyson knew this), and one is aware of many social and philosophical questions in the background that never come into the focus of clear discussion.

In the imaginary story-teller, too, is a characteristic that is 'very Tennysonian indeed', as Miss Pitt remarks. The Prince is taken periodically with 'weird seizures', a trance-like condition where events are still apprehended, yet without any conviction of their reality. It is a kind of dream-state in which the purpose and reality of the day-to-day world fade. The mind begins to swim with uncertainty. 'You—tell us what we are' is a demand that comes sharply and seriously from one of the young ladies in the Conclusion of the poem. She too has been in a thoughtful, abstracted mood, in which all the normal certainties have melted. From Shakespeare's Prospero she might have had the answer, 'We are such stuff as dreams are made on', and that too would be 'very Tennysonian indeed'. For, although no reply to the girl's question is given, a sort of answer comes in the descriptive lines that almost immediately follow:

> we climb'd
> The slope to Vivian Place, and turning saw

The happy valleys half in light, and half
Far-shadowing from the west, a land of peace:
Gray halls alone among their massive groves;
Trim hamlets; here and there a rustic tower
Half-lost in belts of hop and breadths of wheat;
The shimmering glimpses of a stream; the seas;
A red sail, or a white; and far beyond,
Imagined more than seen, the skirts of France.

All that we know about man, his purpose, his place in the
universe (the poem seems to be saying) is as misty as this landscape. But, Tennyson might have continued, something *is* there
and it is worth living to see.

For the spirit of *The Princess* is optimistic; and one does not
feel that Tennyson is being cheerful simply because the critics
told him it was his duty to be. Rather, it reflects the new happiness and stability of his own life. It is worth noting that the
'weird seizures' of the Prince were added for the fourth edition,
of 1851, and that these too find a happy ending. For with Ida's
love comes an end to this 'haunting sense of hollow shows'.
Miss Pitt comments justly: 'We may without hesitation suppose
that Tennyson's marriage (in 1850) did precisely this'. It
brought a new certainty; it established a living relationship in a
way that no friendship since Hallam's death had been able to do.
Tennyson no longer felt himself an isolated mind, but, as Miss
Pitt puts it, 'a public poet'. And perhaps it is no coincidence that
in that very year he felt ready to publish *In Memoriam*. Much
of the dark chaos that Hallam's death had produced in the
private mind had now been manufactured into an orderly form,
a creation and a public possession.

6

'In Memoriam'

'Next to the Bible . . .' (Queen Victoria)

In Memoriam is both a poem and a collection of poems. Each of its 131 sections can be read as a separate piece, yet all of them work together, connected by themes, by the verse form, and by a common source of inspiration in the death of Arthur Hallam.

These two identities are not always peacefully coexistent. Sometimes one feels that the individual poems are limited by having to conform to the rhyming four-line verse-scheme (the form has the merit of imposing a discipline so that emotion cannot spend itself too unrestrainedly; on the other hand, it tends to check the lyrical flow of the verse and to encourage a rather heavy, oracular kind of utterance). But then the poem, seen as a single creation, also suffers, because the parts do not *appear* to be firmly ordered. One cannot readily see that they make a clear progression, or that they group themselves so as to form something comparable to the movements of a symphony, each with its well-defined climax. The words 'appear' and 'readily' need to be emphasised, for many readers have drawn up their own schemes, pointing out where they see the main groupings and the principal climaxes. Unfortunately, they all tend to be different, and this suggests that the searchers are after all looking for something that is not there. Yet Tennyson took very special care over the arranging of *In Memoriam*, and it must have been done to some purpose. A reader is quite aware that some of the poems follow one another in their line of thought and so form a sequence, and that the whole composition begins in grief and ends in hope. Still, its progression is neither a single, uninterrupted, logical line, nor is it one where the writer pauses systematically after a certain climax has been reached so that his reader can take stock of the position and say: 'Yes, *that* has been accomplished; now we're going to look at *this*'. There remains a feeling that, as Tennyson gropes for light in the darkness of his spiritual life, so in the actual form of the poem he moves forward with a certain vagueness of direction. And this, in a work as long as *In Memoriam*, is a disability.

But long poems run into many dangers. They have to avoid the charge of monotony and to do that they must offer a sufficient range and variety. They also have to preserve artistic unity, and if they are not very careful the 'broadened range' will simply be seen as irrelevancy and the variety as out-of-place. Over the years, *In Memoriam* has incurred both criticisms. Even amid the general enthusiasm of its first reception, a few dissident voices were raised. Charlotte Brontë closed the book half-way, saying, 'It is beautiful; it is mournful; it is monotonous'. Mary Mitford, author of *Our Village*, found 'so many poems, all in one measure, and all on one subject . . . tiresome enough'. Edward Fitzgerald wrote to Tennyson's brother Frederick, repeating the complaint of monotony, and adding the deadly and memorable comment that it 'has that air of being evolved by a Poetical Machine of the highest order'. Poor Tennyson! But the critics have not done with him yet, for a modern American writer, Paull F. Baum (*Tennyson Sixty Years After*, University of North Carolina Press, 1948) finds too much variety, or at any rate a 'mixture of incompatible styles'. 'It is only natural', he says, 'that during seventeen years a poet's style should vary, and should vary with the different kinds of subject, but at a sacrifice of unity; in this poem, however, the variations are not so much due to Tennyson's maturing as to his choice of manners.'

Both this charge and the charge of monotony have something to be said for them, though they seem to me to be right in a way that does not matter and wrong in a way that does. Take Mr. Baum's criticism. He gives several instances of what he has in mind. Sections LXXXVI and LXXXVII, for example, are seen

as inharmonious, the style of the first being quite different from
that of the second. The first is short enough to quote in full:

> Sweet after showers, ambrosial air,
>> That rollest from the gorgeous gloom
>> Of evening over brake and bloom
> And meadow, slowly breathing bare
>
> The round of space, and rapt below
>> Thro' all the dewy tassell'd wood,
>> And shadowing down the horned flood
> In ripples, fan my brows and blow
>
> The fever from my cheek, and sigh
>> The full new life that feeds thy breath
>> Throughout my frame, till Doubt and Death,
> Ill brethren, let the fancy fly
>
> From belt to belt of crimson seas
>> On leagues of odour streaming far,
>> To where in yonder orient star
> A hundred spirits whisper 'Peace'.

The second is the poem about Cambridge:

> I past beside the reverend walls
>> In which of old I wore the gown;
>> I roved at random thro' the town,
> And saw the tumult of the halls;

Tennyson goes back to his college, 'Up that long walk of limes
. . . To see the room in which he [Hallam] dwelt':

> Another name was on the door.
>> I linger'd; all within was noise
>> Of songs, and clapping hands, and boys
> That crash'd the glass and beat the floor;

The disharmony of styles that Mr. Baum observes is located in
the phrase 'the gorgeous gloom of evening' from the one poem,
and 'that crash'd the glass' from the other. He himself takes the
point as being self-evident and does not analyse or comment

further. So one has to run the risk of an interpretation. His point, as I take it, is *not* that you can't have gloom and jollity shoulder to shoulder, or as close as they are in these two consecutive poems. It is rather that 'the gorgeous gloom of evening' is a phrase in Tennyson's own personal, romantic style, while 'boys that crash'd the glass' is a kind of expression closer to the eighteenth century, and an example of a style that was by that time old-fashioned. It is as though (one might add this by way of explaining the criticism) a bar of Mozart were suddenly to appear in a piece of Tchaikowsky. But is it? The comparison surely makes Mr. Baum's criticisms of Tennyson seem niggling and exaggerated. For the clash of styles which the critic sees as presented by that second phrase occurs, as far as I can see, through the action of one word only; that is the definite article (boys that crash'd *the* glass). It is a feature of eighteenth century (or 'classical') style that you should somehow generalise such images. 'Their glasses' becomes 'The glass' (as in Gray's *Elegy*, 'a moping owl is complaining to the moon' becomes '*the* moping owl does to the moon complain'). Through the definite article, the individual owl or glass or young man becomes representative of the type. This, of course, is exactly what Tennyson wants. He is saying not merely 'I heard a noise of undergraduates having a party' but also 'the *race* of undergraduates goes on, doing the same things as they did in my day, and as they no doubt will in the future; and the ever-rolling stream of time moves on quite unaffected by my friend's death'. All this is implied in the *manner* of expression that Tennyson adopts here. The manner is the one best suited to convey the meaning, and the meaning is thoroughly germane, 'organic' to the poem as a whole. The example given is only one of several that Mr. Baum provides, but the others are not, to my mind, any more persuasive.

One can more easily sympathise with the criticism of Charlotte Brontë who closed the book half-way; for *In Memoriam* is certainly too much (even for an *un*-'ordinary mortal') to read at one sitting. But a description like 'mournfully monotonous' is not really accurate. 'Ring out, wild bells', cries Section CVI:

> Ring out the old, ring in the new,
>> Ring, happy bells, across the snow:
>> The year is going, let him go;
> Ring out the false, ring in the true.

A poem that has such a paean of happiness and renewal at its heart is not simply 'mournful'. It is true that *In Memoriam* is primarily an elegy, and that if it were a painted picture the canvas would be a dark one. 'Ring out, wild bells' comes as a sudden flash of scarlet colouring, though there are other passages, as in Section CXXII, where light is admitted, where spring and the flowering of new life are not overshadowed:

> And all the breeze of Fancy blows,
>> And every dew-drop paints a bow,
>> The wizard lightnings deeply glow,
> And every thought breaks out a rose.

Now, these are not 'bits of optimism' imported into the poem and put in towards the end so as to show 'the sunshine through the tears' ('every cloud has a silver lining') or to provide an 'uplifting' finale, in the manner we associate with Hollywood. Hopefulness and a strong sense of the good in man and his world have been present from the start. In Section I, Tennyson recognises that there may in the long run be a gain to counterbalance even such a loss as he is mourning. He knows:

> That men may rise on stepping-stones
> Of their dead selves to higher things.

He says that reason knows this may be so, and yet it is hard in the first stages of grief to:

> reach a hand thro' time to catch
> The far-off interest of tears.

In a sense, that is what the whole poem ultimately does, reaching through seventeen years and trying to make this experience of loss yield a settled mind and understanding. As it progresses, the poem takes up all the emotions, doubts and fears that Hallam's death has stimulated. It provides opportunity to face despair by

76

expressing it, and to reaffirm faith by testing it. This reaffirmation will be the 'far-off interest of tears': the gain that loss has made possible. In the meantime, he says, 'Let Love clasp Grief lest both be drown'd'. This is not a morbid statement, I think; nor is 'mournful' quite the word for it, for that suggests something passive. Tennyson's mourning, his writing of these poems, is essentially an expression of love, and therefore positive and active. The strength of love and the intensity of loss, he feels, are exactly proportionate. Sayings like 'mourning won't do you any good' or 'cheer up: you're not the only one in trouble' and 'you've got other friends left' are all very sensible and all very inadequate (Section VI):

> common is the commonplace
> And vacant chaff well meant for grain.

Instead of easing your feelings in these ways, he believes that you should be honest and give full recognition to all that you have lost. Tennyson's feeling here is like Rickie's in E. M. Forster's novel, *The Longest Journey*. A girl has just learnt of her fiancé's death, and Rickie, whose emotions are also much involved in the situation, talks to her:

> It's the worst thing that can ever happen to you in all your life and you've got to mind it—you've got to mind it. They'll come saying, 'Bear up—trust to time'. No, no; they're wrong. Mind it.

Rickie has seen this love affair as a sudden illumination; something by which the vision of life and its possibilities had suddenly been set alight. If one is to lose such happiness, the loss must be fully experienced as tragic, no less. Otherwise what seems deep and marvellous in folk is only idle and ephemeral after all; and if so, the cynics are right, we humans are a poor breed and the 'love' we boast of as a noble thing is only Time's fool, an intense infatuation, not much more. Hence Tennyson's 'Let Love clasp Grief lest both be drown'd'. It is to Love as a still-living reality that the poem constantly turns; and with this in mind, one cannot really use 'mournful' as an adequate description.

'Monotonous' involves a different kind of critical comment. If people say 'This is monotonous' they generally mean 'This bores me' and as a piece of autobiography the saying cannot be contradicted. The statement becomes literary criticism only when reasons, based on observation, are added to it. So when Miss Mitford said that the monotony arises from there being 'so many poems, all in one measure, and all on one subject', she provided some grounds for critical discussion. For example: the poems *are* 'all in one measure' to the extent that the same verse form is used throughout, but within that form there is still much variation. The pauses within the lines, the run-on of one line into the next, sometimes of one verse into the next, all give variation to the movement. In this way neither rhyme nor rhythm becomes too insistent; the regular 'thud' of emphasis is avoided, and the poem moves like a piece of music in which the time signature is constant, while rhythmic interest is maintained by varied phrasing. LXXXVI (printed on p. 74) shows the verse at its most flexible. If written out in free verse, or in a way that would tell the reader where to pause, it might look like this:

> Sweet after showers,
> Ambrosial air,
> That rollest from the gorgeous gloom of evening
> Over brake and bloom and meadow,
> Slowly breathing bare
> The round of space,
> And rapt below through all the dewy-tassell'd wood,
> And shadowing down the horned flood in ripples,
> Fan my brows
> And blow the fever from my cheek,
> And sigh the full new life that feeds thy breath
> Throughout my frame,
> Till Doubt and Death,
> Ill brethren,
> Let the fancy fly from belt to belt of crimson seas
> On leagues of odour streaming far,
> To where in yonder orient star
> A hundred spirits
> Whisper 'Peace'.

The rhymes make their addition to the music, yet one is hardly aware of them. Nothing thumps; the movement forward is felt delicately but insistently, corresponding with the freshening buoyancy and gentle power of the wind. Variety of 'measure', then, is present to a remarkable degree.

The monotony of 'so many poems, all in one measure' was one complaint; the other was that the poems are 'all on one subject'. I think that if I had not read the poem, but merely knew of it, I should gather from this that it was simply a collection of 131 laments for the same person. In a sense they *are* 'all on one subject', and rightly so, for in an artistic work some unity of theme is wanted. But that subject can hardly be defined as 'the death of Arthur Hallam in 1833'. Let us look at some of the sections. Section I is about grief as the measure of love; II places the life of a man, so insignificant in time, against other inanimate parts of creation; III wonders whether there is sense or purpose in creation at all, and is perplexed to find the mind possessed by such doubts; IV looks inward and, relaxing from the tense anxiety of disbelief, acknowledges that unhappiness has numbed the will, though the poet believes that this cannot last for ever; V expresses the comfort which the making of these poems gives. The sixth section gives a series of pictures (very Victorian ones) of other people in sudden loss, so that Tennyson's own situation can be seen as representative: he is, in fact, deliberately broadening the scope and application of his elegy. Some of the sections express thoughts and feelings aroused at different times of the year such as Christmas and the anniversaries of Hallam's death; and constantly present is the background of seasonal change which is linked (though not by any crude and over-explicit symbolism) to the development in the poet's soul. The poem also includes some references to family events: leaving the house at Somersby; the visit of Tennyson's brother Charles to Europe; the marriage of his youngest sister Cecilia and his friend Edmund Lushington. Again the scope is broadened. Tennyson said that the poem 'begins with a funeral and ends with a marriage', and so it embraces as its subject-matter much of fundamental human experience. Miss Mitford complained that there are 'so many poems, all on one subject'; but when the 'subject' is as broad and deep as this, a poet may well hope to write at some length without incurring the charge of monotony.

We are coming now, however, to a point where criticisms do seem to be valid. For the scope of *In Memoriam* sometimes exceeds what Tennyson could achieve. He wanted, above all things, to find and give reasons for hope. 'Hope' for him meant faith, and faith meant believing in God's existence, His benevolent purpose for mankind, and His gift of eternal life to those who have deserved it. All are vital issues in the poem, the last especially, and it is in this that Tennyson's limitations are most felt. He had in fact changed from the days of the *Supposed Confessions* (see pp. 49-50) and real faith had become more difficult to him. A kind of desperation about his need for faith undermines his position from first to last. In Section XXXIV he writes:

> My own dim life should teach me this,
>   That Life shall live for evermore,
>   Else earth is darkness at the core,
> And dust and ashes all that is.

But this is the worst kind of argument. 'There must be a life after death,' he is saying, 'because life would be too bad to bear if there were not'.

> 'Twere best at once to sink to peace,
>   Like birds the charming serpent draws,
>   To drop head-foremost in the jaws
> Of vacant darkness and to cease.

'I shall despair if I don't believe; therefore I must believe' is the argument. But this sort of desperate need for faith implies of itself that it isn't there: that doubt remains even in the very act of saying that one must not doubt. Sir Charles Tennyson records, in his *Alfred Tennyson*, that much later in life his grandfather said:

> 'If there is a God that has made the earth and put this hope and passion in us, it must be the truth. If it be not true, then no God but a mocking fiend created us and (flushing crimson with

excitement) I'd shake my fist in his almighty face and tell him that I cursed him—I'd sink my head straight in a chloroformed handkerchief and have done with it all.'

This does not impress one as being the language of a settled, faithful mind.

It might be objected that Section XXXIV is early in the sequence and that faith is more strenuously affirmed later; that the experiences recorded later in the poem themselves help to promote a stronger faith than this. Section CXXIV would be an instance:

> If e'er when faith had fall'n asleep,
>   I heard a voice 'believe no more'
>   And heard an ever-breaking shore
> That tumbled in the Godless deep;
>
> A warmth within the breast would melt
>   The freezing reason's colder part,
>   And like a man in wrath the heart
> Stood up and answer'd, 'I have felt'.

The trouble is that Tennyson *tells* us this without communicating it; we have to take it on trust through statement instead of sharing the experience through poetry. There is also something over-assertive about this heart which stands up 'like a man in wrath': a too self-consciously majestic dignity. It comes too near to posturing, even though the three simple words, 'I have felt', ought in themselves to speak with a serene and unanswerable authority.

The tone of *In Memoriam*, then, has not the gentle firmness of a man who has come through his spiritual troubles. The balance in the mind is probably truthfully represented not by the assertiveness of CXXIV but by the anxious, almost plaintive, hopefulness of the Introductory Section (written in 1849):

> Strong Son of God, immortal Love,
>   Whom we, that have not seen thy face,
>   By faith, and faith alone, embrace,
> Believing where we cannot prove . . .

Thou wilt not leave us in the dust:
  Thou madest man, he knows not why,
  He thinks he was not made to die,
And thou hast made him; thou art just.

There is, on balance, a sincere trust here; yet we still sense the undercurrent of anxiety. It is almost a plea, almost (oddly) an attempt to prove by a logic that *must* make eternal life a truth: even, still more oddly, a humble attempt to browbeat God with logic. 'You made man; Your creation believes that he will live again after death; You are just': these three statements are the premises from which a deduction is to be made. The deduction is, of course, that a just God would not disappoint man in his most heart-felt wish. What follows from this is that if there is no eternal life then there is something wrong with one of the premises—and the one which would be most in question is God's justice. So again, very strangely, there are evidences of doubt even where faith is most genuinely expressed. Even where humility is most sincere, the soul stands with the greatest dignity and with a challenging moral authority before its creator. Even at the very moment of saying that he believes where he cannot prove, he does the very opposite: attempts to prove where he cannot quite completely believe. For the stresses and strains of his troubled heart we must have respect; more than respect, indeed, because by his art he draws us into exceptionally close sympathy. But he was, at certain points vital to his thinking (and to his self-knowledge), a strangely muddled man. And there is something in G. M. Young's dictum (*Victorian England*, p. 75): 'In his highest mood, Tennyson sometimes speaks like an archangel assuring the universe that it will muddle through'.

We may perhaps ask why nineteenth-century England needed any assurances on that score. Wasn't this the supreme age of complacency and confidence in the inevitability of progress? That is certainly the conception of the nineteenth century that used to be current, and it is partly true. But every great Victorian writer (perhaps Browning alone excepted) was worried about some feature of the age. Apart from being a complacent period, it was also 'The Age of Reform'; in the face of much opposition and indifference, there were enough conscientious public men to effect more social and political change in ten years than eighteenth-century government had brought about in a hundred. Each reform implied the recognition that some part of the *status quo* was defective; which in turn implies a critical spirit and not a complacent one. Their *long-term* complacency was much more deeply grounded. They did believe that more votes for more people, along with more education for more voters, would be the means to 'the golden future time'. They believed in England, and in its strength which lay in both material and moral responsibility to the rest of the world. And behind all this was a faith that God, 'working His purpose out as year succeeds to year', had a hand in history, or at any rate that if man submitted his will to God's then the divine plan for progress would become manifest. For man was the apple of God's eye, created in God's own image, as Genesis says, and naturally God wanted the species to prosper.

But here came a doubt and a difficulty. For if it should be found that man was not a special creation, then the idea that God had a particular interest in him becomes harder to accept. This is just what the nineteenth century did find out, and *In Memoriam* shows Tennyson deeply troubled by it.

Darwin's *Origin of Species* did not appear till 1859, and many of the sections of *In Memoriam* which show some understanding of the idea of evolution and of the implication of other biological studies date back to the 'thirties. Darwin's book is of course the most famous biological treatise, and it is commonly held to have been the prime disturber of faith in the nineteenth century. It was quite against the author's wish that this should have been so. Tennyson himself met Darwin, who called to visit him at Farringford in 1868. Mrs. Tennyson records: 'Alfred said to him, "Your theory of Evolution does not make against Christianity" and Darwin answered, "No, certainly not" '. But many

---

* Samuel Butler read this and copied it into a notebook, commenting, 'How well both Tennyson and Darwin knew that he was lying!'

people felt that it did. If over an untold expanse of time some kind of ape-like creature changed by imperceptible degrees into a being recognisable as man, then it has to be accepted that the account in Genesis of man's creation is, at the very least, a misleading one:

> And the Lord God formed man of the dust of the ground, and breathed into his nostrils the breath of life; and man became a living soul.

According to Genesis, moreover, this soul and the body it inhabited were made 'in the image of God'. The idea of evolution does not preclude the possibility that 'completed' man may still be 'the image of God', but the creation of man cannot be said to have happened as a special separate act. This need not destroy anyone's faith, but it does very radically affect man's conception of himself as a species. No longer a special creation, he becomes historically and biologically simply a part of the animal life that has populated the world for a part of the world's existence. Man's dignity takes a severe tumble. When, in the Middle Ages, man could see himself at the centre of all creation (the planets revolving round the earth of which he was king), then it seemed logical and fitting that man should be the special care of his creator. The first blow to that came when the astronomers put the sun in the centre, and earth, now insignificant in the scheme of things, out into space. The second came when the biologists put man among the animals, showing him to be subject to the same evolutionary process as the rest of animal life, neither the first lord of creation nor necessarily the last. That God should take a special interest in *this* creature (let alone in all the individuals belonging to the species) was somewhat harder to believe.

All this is reflected in *In Memoriam*. Tennyson asks (LV) whether the belief in life after death may be a delusion. The idea, he says, surely comes to us from God, but why should we believe that such special care should be taken of us when we look around at nature and see no care taken of individual lives at all?

Are God and Nature then at strife,
  That Nature lends such evil dreams?
  So careful of the type she seems,
So careless of the single life.

Then, in the next Section (LVI) he reflects that even this is not really true of nature:

'So careful of the type?' but no.
  From scarped cliff and quarried stone
  She cries, 'A thousand types are gone:
I care for nothing; all shall go'.

Whole species are eventually destroyed, species (as the geologists were showing) whose existence on earth was quite as long as man's has so far been. Why should we assume that there is one law for the rest of nature and another specially for us?

These were some of the thoughts that weighed heavily with Tennyson. Others were possibly more disturbing still. For, after all, God may still have a purpose for man and it may still be a good one, answering the heart's desire, as long as God is Himself good. But what do we learn of the Creator from His creation? The Victorians inherited a habit of thinking in this way, for it had been a way of thought dear to theologians and philosophers since the Middle Ages. 'Every creature is a written letter declaring Goodness', said Raymond de Sabunde in the sixteenth century, representing mediaeval orthodoxy. And in the eighteenth century at Cambridge, Archdeacon Paley had exclaimed: 'It is a happy world after all. The air, the earth, the water teem with delighted existence'. But Tennyson had different thoughts when he looked at nature:

For Nature is one with rapine, a harm no preacher can heal;
The Mayfly is torn by the swallow, the sparrow spear'd by the shrike,
And the whole little wood where I sit is a world of plunder and prey.

That comes from *Maud* (Part I, 4, 4), written in 1856. But the thought is an expansion of the famous phrase in *In Memoriam*:

'Nature, red in tooth and claw' (LVI). What conclusion can the moralist draw from this side of nature? He cannot do much more than ask the question 'Are God and Nature then at strife?', as Tennyson does. For unless one admits the possibility of a God who is somehow not in full control of matter ('at war with Nature'), one is left with unwelcome choices: either God is not (by our standards) good; or He is impersonal and quite apart from a world created experimentally; or He does not exist.

All these unpleasant reflections stir uneasily in the back of the mind. As the century advanced, more people were to be worried by them and were to accept one of the unpleasant conclusions. Tennyson did not. He let the reflections simmer a little more, then put them away from his mind (or at least from the mind that was willing to express itself—for he did many years later acknowledge to Sir James Knowles, that *In Memoriam* was too hopeful, 'More than I am myself'); and he again humbly and hopefully asserted that he would believe (LV):

> I stretch lame hands of faith, and grope,
>   And gather dust and chaff, and call
>   To what I feel is Lord of all,
> And faintly trust the larger hope.

G. M. Young comments: '*In Memoriam* is one of the cardinal documents of the mid-Victorian mind, its ardent curiosity, its exquisite sensitiveness to nature, and, not less, perhaps, its unwillingness to quit, and its incapacity to follow, any chain of reasoning which seems likely to result in an unpleasant conclusion'.

The last clauses of that sentence are perhaps a little hard. Tennyson did at this stage follow the chain of reasoning much more closely than did most of his contemporaries. He was well in advance of most in being aware of evolution at all. Darwin's precursors were Lamarck, Buffon (whose work was in Dr. Tennyson's library at Somersby) and Sir Charles Lyell (whose *Principles of Geology* Tennyson read in 1837). Tennyson and his group at Cambridge discussed kindred problems in the late twenties, and we can guess from *The Supposed Confessions of a*

Second-Rate Sensitive Mind that the intellectual objection Tennyson was familiar with at that time included some of the uneasy speculations set free by the biologists. He seems in fact to have followed the arguments and their implications with unusually clear understanding. If he did not then allow himself to come to the logical but unpleasant conclusions it was because he did not believe that 'logical conclusions' were necessarily the truth. Human reasoning is fallible; brilliant discoveries and clever theories can lead straight to hell. He would still do his best to believe, and in the meantime would console himself with that thought that (XCVI):

> There lives more faith in honest doubt,
> Believe me, than in half the creeds.

The position has its dignity, and it even took a little courage to adopt it. The lines just quoted were held by some to be dangerous and heretical. A popular religious journal, the *Christian Remembrancer*, had said of Tennyson after the publication of *The Princess*: 'No one would call him a Christian poet'; and *In Memoriam* only confirmed their view of the matter.

Tennyson's rewards were many, however. The poem sold at a great rate (it was published in June, and 5,000 had gone by September). It was praised as 'the solace and delight of every house where poetry is loved'. More than that, it gave delight and, later, solace at Osborne and Windsor. The Prince Consort admired it sufficiently to intervene on Tennyson's behalf when his name came up, fourth in the list, as a candidate for the post of Poet Laureate. And twelve years later, as the Queen stood with 'a kind of stately innocence' before Tennyson himself, she said, 'Next to the Bible *In Memoriam* is my comfort'. Many other Victorians could quite sincerely have said the same: and the tribute should not leave us unimpressed.

7

'Maud' and Farringford

'He sits at home by his own snug hearth, and hears the storm howl without' ('Anti-Maud')

1850 brought marriage and honour. Tennyson married the long-beloved Emily Sellwood and succeeded Wordsworth as Poet Laureate. The next years brought children, a valued home, and new friends. One might have expected, therefore, that the 1855 volume of poetry would be a happy one, reflecting a new confidence and warmth; less personal, maybe, more outward-looking; possibly heavier with the consciousness of public position and moral responsibility. How surprising, then, that the major work in this volume should have been a study in neurosis bordering on madness, and that on publication it should have proved itself very largely an offence to public and critics alike. That, however, was the character and the fate of *Maud*, the poem for which Tennyson had probably the greatest affection of all, and the one in which later ages have taken probably the most lively interest.

Maud has been called 'the antiphonal voice to *In Memoriam*', which seems to imply a comparison rather than a contrast. Both poems are the sustained expression of serious and largely unhappy states of mind. Both strike one as being to a great extent personal (though this is something that will require discussion). Both trace a spiritual progress into the heart of darkness from which they emerge with some positive assertions of faith and purpose. But a contrast also has to be made. For while *In Memoriam* maintains dignity and control even in its most troubled expressions of doubt and grief, *Maud* voices a black, raging despair and, with it, a kind of ecstasy that is almost equally beyond the control of reason. This contrast is made more forcible by the differences of technique. In *In Memoriam* the unity of verse-form helps to control the emotion; by contrast with *Maud* this is a classical, regulated expression, submitting itself to a fairly rigorous discipline imposed by metre and rhythm. *Maud*, however, recognises no law of composition: it is a medley of styles and forms, the verses varying in response to the mood. This gives free rein to the moodiness of the narrator, the 'I' of the poem; and so, in a much more romantic, undisciplined way, the poem can be an expression of personality, raging in a fierce, exclamatory kind of verse, swooning ecstatically in long lines or tripping along daintily in short ones as the mood takes it. T. S. Eliot has observed of *In Memoriam* that it has the character of a diary: it records experiences as they happen, thoughts as they occur. *Maud* is still more diary-like. With a greater effect of spontaneity, capturing vividly the excitement of a solitary man who returns from an encounter and in the full warmth of his emotions writes of it in his private book, this poem goes much further in establishing a sense of intimate personal contact; and because so much depends on the character with whom we have this contact (for the 'I' of the poem is not necessarily the poet), the poem itself remains eccentric. *In Memoriam* speaks to us, across the gap of a hundred years, from a position at the centre of the Victorian world picture. *Maud* is still a nineteenth-century grotesque: a vivid, often beautiful freak.

It is none the less Tennysonian for that. Indeed, recent researches have suggested a closely personal, even autobiographical involvement, and the poem has been claimed as 'a crucial document' in Tennyson's biography. This involves what is certainly a crux in any critical discussion: the question of how far Tennyson is identified with the 'I' of the poem, and how far he is creating a character as a dramatist might, objectively and in dissociation.

Maud is described in the sub-title as 'a Monodrama', a form half-way between play and dramatic monologue. We are spectators at a sequence of events; or rather, we see them, as in the off-stage happenings of a Greek tragedy, through the eyes of a narrator. What we view at first hand is the narrator's mind. *Maud* is a play, all soliloquies; or, perhaps, a sequence of connected sketches performed by one of those highly-skilled artists (like Ruth Draper of a generation or two ago) who can stand on the stage alone and fill it with objects and people all invisible yet magically vivid. But the centre of interest remains the speaker himself, and if we are to go further than merely finding an 'interest', we must be able to feel a strong sympathy with him. The poem can have a powerful emotional effect, but only, I think, if the 'I' is felt as a character whom we can like and pity. When Tennyson read it aloud, the tears flowed freely: 'Wonderful, tender, beautiful, and he read exquisitely in a voice like an organ, rather than speech,' wrote Elizabeth Barrett-Browning. It is also notable that through these readings, Tennyson's listeners came to feel a much greater liking for the character of the hero than they had known before. Everything here (the emotional power of the poem once sympathy is accorded, and the great feeling that Tennyson himself had for it) suggests an unusual closeness between author and character. And if this is so, then some of the criticisms which the Victorians levelled at the poem are not so wide of the mark as has often been suggested.

The hostility to *Maud* had several causes. One of them was the quite genuine difficulty of dealing with an unfamiliar kind of writing. Tennyson makes his reader work. We are not always told in so many words what has happened or where we are: the fact of Maud's death, for example, is not made explicit, but has to be conjectured. The charge of 'obscurity mistaken for profundity' was not a surprising one under the circumstances. But it is not this line of attack that concerns us here. The other criticism (and this is the more damaging and interesting one) is represented by the phrase 'a vulgar war-whoop'. That comes from a poem called *Anti-Maud*, a clever parody written in 1855 by W. C. Bennett, sold in pamphlet form for sixpence, and strongly attacking Tennyson as an armchair warmonger. The

National Review said: 'No prominence to the cause and principle involved can make war a duty and a blessing. In so doing he [Tennyson] is echoing back and furthering one of the evils of a war—the danger that it should be loved for its own sake.'

Now there is no doubt that the character, the 'I' of *Maud*, is open to this charge. His attitude is very like that of Rupert Brooke who could welcome the 1914 war as a cleansing influence. The soldiers went, he said:

> as swimmers into cleanness leaping,
> Glad from a world grown old and cold and weary.

In *Maud* (Part III), the hero has come through a time of great crisis and after suffering agonies of despair when he seems to see no point in living, he finds:

> a hope for the world in the coming wars.

These were the years of the Crimean War:

> And now by the side of the Black and the Baltic deep,
> And dreadful-grinning mouths of the fortress, flames
> The blood-red blossom of war with a heart of fire.

The lines are spoken not with horror but with relish. War gives a purpose to life which peace did not provide, and though he is aware that many innocent folk will be 'crush'd in the clash of jarring claims', he nevertheless finds this preferable to 'a peace that was full of wrongs and shames'. War brings a sense of brotherhood, of fellowship in the common cause. He stands on the 'giant deck' of a battleship going out to the Crimea and feels the excitement of mixing his breath:

> With a loyal people shouting a battle-cry.

There is even a mystical feeling of being taken up in God's own hand, being made an active part of the Divine Scheme, losing individuality in race-consciousness and surrendering the individual will to the movement of 'Destiny':

> I have felt with my native land, I am one with my kind,
> I embrace the purpose of God, and the doom assign'd·

All of this has a more sinister sound in our century than it had in Tennyson's own. The idea that the best comes out of man 'under the red reign of war' was powerfully urged by Mussolini and Hitler. The emotional attractiveness of feeling oneself part of a huge patriotic movement ('a loyal people shouting a battle-cry') was so exactly what Hitler's mass-rallies exploited that we must look at it all with suspicion and distaste. When we read Brooke's lines about soldiers 'as swimmers into cleanness leaping', we marvel bitterly that such a thing could ever have been said, and as we read the history of the Crimean War with its incalculable suffering and wastage, the exultant welcome given to it in *Maud* registers as idealistic silliness of a particularly dangerous kind. To this extent the strong reaction against *Maud* is to the Victorians' credit.

But, of course, Tennyson had a ready answer. It was that the hero of *Maud* was not to be taken for Tennyson himself, and that the hero's attitude to war was not necessarily the poet's own. 'The mistake that people make', said Tennyson, 'is that they think the poet's poems are a kind of *catalogue raisonné* of his very own self, and of all the facts of his life, not seeing that they often only express a poetic instinct, or judgement on character real or imagined.' This is what one would like to believe. One would like to be able to see *Maud* as an objective, imaginative exploration into a neurotic, diseased mind, in which the 'solution' that the character finds to his troubles is itself part of the disease. This would be possible, for as a psychological 'case' the hero of *Maud* is thoroughly consistent and credible. It is quite consistent that he should *think* he has found a solution to his own troubles and to the world's, when in reality he is pursuing a romantic illusion, licking a sweet that is his (and the world's) poison. The trouble is, there is too little evidence that Tennyson saw it that way. On the contrary, all the biographical evidence as well as the feeling of the poem suggests that Tennyson saw in the last part of *Maud* the regeneration of his hero and a source of inspiration to his countrymen.

Regeneration, national and moral, is an important theme in *Maud*. The need for it is acutely felt throughout. Introverted, self-pitying and unstable as he is, the hero of *Maud* is neverthe-less a telling social critic. Tennyson certainly stands behind his character when he is denouncing the evils of commercialism and the industrial towns (Part I, *1*, 9 and 10):

> When the poor are hovell'd and hustled together, each sex, like
>   swine . . .
> And the vitriol madness flushes up in the ruffian's head,
> Till the filthy by-lane rings to the yell of the trampled wife,
> And chalk and alum and plaster are sold to the poor for bread
> And the spirit of murder works in the very means of life.

Capitalism, he sees (Part I, *1 o*, 1), has brought with it conditions of servitude where wealth is made for the mine-owner by:

> Grimy nakedness dragging his trucks
> And laying his trams in a poison'd gloom.

Nor does so much sweated labour contribute to a fine way of life even for the class that profits from it. Instead, the commercial motive is everywhere, poisoning life and making peace a mockery (Part I, *1*, 6 and 7):

> Why do they prate of the blessings of peace? we have made them
>   a curse,.
> Pickpockets, each hand lusting for all that is not its own;
> And lust of gain, in the spirit of Cain, is it better or worse
> Than the heart of the citizen hissing in war on his own hearth-
>   stone? . . .
> Is it peace or war? Civil war, as I think, and that of a kind
> The viler, as underhand, not openly bearing the sword

This much is trenchant social criticism and, allowing for rhetorical exaggeration, it is also just.

Tennyson's own sympathy for the poor, and indignation at their condition, had been aroused a few years earlier by his reading of the novel *Alton Locke* (1850) and his friendship with its author, Charles Kingsley. In spite of Kingsley's socialism, the two men had much in common: a hatred for commercialism, for the 'shopkeepers', the Manchester Radicals, and a hope that national salvation might be found through an alliance between the working people, the gentry, and the Church. In *Alton Locke* one can see a good deal that went into the mind which was to produce *Maud*. 'It was a' poison in London', says a character called Sandy Mackaye: 'Bread full o' alum and bones, and sic filth'. 'The tyrant Mammon' is a recurrent phrase (cf. *Maud*, Part I, *i*, 12: 'When a Mammonite mother kills her babe for a burial fee, And Timour-Mammon grins on a pile of children's bones'). Kingsley also develops the notion that the 'peace' of our civilisation is a fraud. So many men are at war with each other in the cut-throat world of competition in business, and for so many others the 'peace' is simply a perpetual fight to keep alive. So he attacks newspaper writers who are 'prophesying smooth things to Mammon, crying in daily leaders, "Peace! peace!" when there is no peace' (cf. *Maud*, Part I, *i*, 7: 'Is it peace or war? Civil war, as I think'). Money, in Kingsley's novel as in Tennyson's poem, is the great tyrant of England. Principles go overboard at the dictates of commercial interest. One might expect Liberals, for example, to sympathise with the revolutions against despotism in Europe, but no. ' "Revolutions interfered with trade!" and therefore they were damnable! . . . No, it was with the profits of the few that revolutions interfered; with the divine right, not so much of kings, but of money making. They hampered Mammon, the very fiend who is devouring the masses.' This same fiend, in *Maud*, is represented as being England's false god, and the narrator (Part III, *i*, 2) looks forward to a time when:

> The glory of manhood (shall) stand on his ancient height,
> Nor Britain's one sole God be the millionaire.
> No more shall commerce be all in all.

In this much, the narrator's opinions are almost certainly Tennyson's also. They correspond both with the feelings of Kingsley's novel, a book that evidently made a great impression on him, for there are many other signs of its influence in *Maud*, and with his own feelings as expressed elsewhere (see a note on *Maud and Alton Locke* at the end of this chapter).

A further degree of closeness between Tennyson and the hero of *Maud* is suggested in a recent study called *Tennyson's Maud, The Biographical Genesis* by R. W. Rader. Mr. Rader argues that *Maud* is 'an autobiographical expression', and he shows convincingly that there are many connections between the poem and events in Tennyson's life. The narrator's father, for instance, would 'rage in his mood'—'Ah God, as he used to rage', much as did Tennyson's own father. In Maud's father, the 'old man now lord of the broad estate and the Hall', are several affinities with Tennyson's grandfather; and in the Hall itself, 'gilt with the hand of a millionaire', is a suggestion of both Bayons Manor and Brancepeth Castle, ostentatious homes of richer branches of the family. Maud, Mr. Rader believes, is 'an image in which were blended Tennyson's memories of all three of the women whom he had successively loved'. This is probably the most important part of his book, for if its theory is correct it adds another chapter to Tennyson's biography.

In about 1825 Tennyson met Rosa Baring, the daughter of a wealthy neighbour living at Harrington Hall, some two miles from Somersby Rectory. The relationship probably continued till 1836, when Tennyson wrote an unpublished poem called *To Rosa*, which concerns a lovers' quarrel at a ball (the poem is printed in Mr. Rader's book, and in H. D. Rawnsley's *Memories of the Tennysons*, 1912). There are other poems which fairly certainly refer to Rosa Baring, and Mr. Rader believes that *The Gardener's Daughter* (her name was Rose) also expresses Tennyson's rapturous love for this girl, a love that he came in later years to condemn as a sensual infatuation. The evidence for all this is by no means complete, but the hypothesis is well supported. Rosa Baring, apparently, always believed that the 'rose of the rosebud garden of girls', in *Maud*, had reference to her. In 1837 it was rumoured that she was to be engaged to another man. Tennyson left Somersby in November, probably jealous and wounded in spirit, and it was probably about this time that he wrote *Locksley Hall*. Now *Locksley Hall*, in which an embittered lover is again the narrator, has close kinship with *Maud*, and the conclusion one draws is that both poems embody a good deal of the author's own anger and frustration arising during the 'thirties and continuing to poison his life through the next decade as well.

Of the two other women who may be represented by the character of Maud, one was Emily Sellwood, who after a frustratingly long and broken engagement became Tennyson's wife. The other was Sophy Rawnsley, the girl who is believed to be the original of the early (and intolerable) poem *Airy, fairy Lilian*. Village gossip had it that Tennyson once proposed to her, and it seems that he was strongly attracted by her liveliness and gaiety. Her clear, sensible nature contrasted with Rosa's passionate, sensual character, yet it too lacked something of depth and nobility. The two women, Mr. Rader suggests, stood in Tennyson's mind for two distinct types of human being, and the rose and the lily were their respective symbols in his poetry. So in one of his very late poems, *The Ancient Sage*, Tennyson is writing partly with his own love affairs in mind in the lines:

> The years that when my youth began
>   Had set the lily and rose
> By all my ways where'er they ran,
>   Have ended mortal foes;
> My rose of love for ever gone,
>   My lily of truth and trust—
> They made her lily and rose in one,
>   And changed her into dust.
> O rose-tree planted in my grief,
>   And growing on her tomb,
> Her dust is greening in your leaf,
>   Her blood is in your bloom.
> O slender lily waving there,
>   And laughing back the light,
> In vain you tell me 'Earth is fair'
>   When all is dark as night.

Similarly in *Maud*, Mr. Rader believes, there is an autobiographical reference when Maud, who has been associated with rose and lily at various points in the poem, is described as 'Queen lily and rose in one'. Her nature has the beauties of both girls, and the deficiencies of neither. She is in fact virtually 'true womanhood' as Tennyson found it in Emily Sellwood. 'The peace of God came into my life before the altar when I married her', said Tennyson years later. The hero of *Maud* was never so fortunate: he did not come to the altar and if he found the peace of God at all it was through warfare. But in creating him, Tennyson has relived much of his own life: his family troubles, his loves and private sufferings. As *In Memoriam* expressed all the disturbance, emotional and intellectual, which Hallam's death brought with it, so in *Maud* Tennyson expressed the joys and sorrows he had known through love. Both, then, are very personal poems, and it begins to look as though *Maud* is after all the more personal of the two. 'Biographically', says Mr. Rader, '*Maud* is a crucial document.' He calls it 'a recapitulation of the inner and outer circumstances of his tortured early life, a deeply rooted act of spiritual self-definition and affirmation by which, after the commitment initiated by marriage and the Laureateship, he moved from his earlier to his later career; it is the swan song of the bitter and troubled young poet, the inaugural hymn of the Laureate'.

All told, then, there seems to be a large measure of identification between Tennyson and the character he has created in the narrator. When he defended himself from the charge of war-mongering, saying that it was a mistake to assume that the author thought as this character thought, he was no doubt being quite sincere; I can believe that he hardly suspected how much of himself was in what he had written. His own conscious endeavour would be to create character, situation and verse that should ring true. Accordingly he had peopled his Monodrama vividly. Maud and the narrator play their parts against a background in which others come momentarily but memorably into the light:

> a waxen face,
> A rabbit mouth that is ever agape.   (I, *10, 2*)

> the snowy-banded, dilettante,
> Delicate-handed priest.   (I, *8*)

　　　　that dandy-despot, he,
That jewell'd mass of millinery,
That oil'd and curl'd Assyrian bull,
Smelling of musk and of insolence.　　　(I, 6, 6)

　　　　a glimpse of his face,
A gray old wolf and a lean.　　　(I, 13, 3)

Tennyson also has created a real world for the drama to be set against. The wood, with its red-rimmed hollow; the garden, the stream, the Hall; later the cobbled streets of a Breton town, and the basement 'a yard beneath the street': all are vividly present, parts of a conscientious artistic creation. During the process of composition his mind would have been essentially involved in this: not self-expression, but creation. It is not likely that he would be conscious of half the personal impulses and experiences that were guiding the creation, and he must have thought it exasperatingly naïve of his critics to assume that the narrator of *Maud* was a mere 'front', a mouthpiece for the poet's own opinions. But in a deeper way than was probably suspected by those critics or by himself, he was 'giving of his own substance' in this poem. And I think that when the hero reckons he (and the world) can find regeneration in the battles of the Crimea, there is a basic flaw in the value-judgements not only of the character but of the author too.

Does this affect the *artistic* merit of the work? Many would say it does not. 'This is basically a disagreement over a point of view,' the argument might go. 'He thinks war cleanses; you disagree. You may be right, but you've got to suspend disagreements of this kind if you want to judge a work of art.' To this, the reply might come (and it obviously involves a much broader debate on the whole nature of literature and literary criticism): 'If you continually suspend judgement over subjects like this, you reduce art to the status of an ornament. It becomes a mere elegance, a connoisseur's luxury, rather than something that is at the centre of your thought and feeling. Tennyson here wishes to present his character as being regenerated through war, and there is a strong suggestion that a war would help to cleanse the whole nation, too. When he concerns himself with national and individual regeneration he is undertaking a subject for which at this stage in his career he has no capacity.' I should myself be on the side of the second speaker in that debate (provided he made it clear that his judgement on poetry involved a great many other considerations too). But in this particular instance, there may be call for a third point of view. 'If we look at *Maud* as an object, a work of art with an existence complete in itself and independent of its author's (so this third voice might argue), shall we not say that it is remarkably consistent and convincing as a psychological study? If we knew nothing else of Tennyson, except the fact that he had originally entitled his poem *The Madness*, should we not see the hero's idealistic nonsense about war as being part of the madness? It is entirely consistent that the man who, before his breakdown, had so despised the present peace, had so longed for something which would give his life purpose and for a strong leader to direct it (Part I, *10*, 5), should now welcome the war, when it came, as a way to free himself from his morbid, passive imprisonment in self. The 'solution' is part of the diseased mentality. The poem presents 'the madness', national and individual, from first to last: this is what it accomplishes. That is what those particular words in that particular order do for us. The accident that we happen to know something about the author does not alter those words and that order. Whatever the author's intentions may have been (and we can never really know this), he has presented us with a remarkably vivid and interesting character in this narrator. If he had devised a 'satisfactory' form of regeneration, then we might have had cause to complain, for the man is clearly too deeply neurotic to make for himself anything that we might regard as a healthy solution. As it is, Tennyson is consistent and we have no reason for criticism.'

I must leave the reader to make up his own mind on the rival claims of my three voices. But as we have stressed the personal involvement of Tennyson in the poem and the character of the narrator, it would be unfair to leave *Maud* without giving credit for objective characterisation too. The accents of madness are well caught (perhaps learnt from observation at Dr. Allen's asylum), and particularly well-done is a kind of high-pitched excitement, with an odd mixture of naïvety and cunning in its exaltation. This, I think, is the tone of the section starting 'Birds in the high Hall-garden' (Part I, 12). This sounds from the first line as though it is to be a lyric in a straightforward manner, comparable, say, to the lyrics in *The Princess* or to 'Go not, happy day' in *Maud*. But in fact it is not this kind of lyric at all; it is not one that can be extracted from the poem, and it is not a resting-place in the narrative. Instead, it takes the story forward and is very much a composition 'in character'. The narrator's voice speaks in its characteristic manner, but with a note of rather feverish excitement that is new to the poem.

> Where was Maud? in our wood:
> And I—who else?—was with her.

There is an odd kind of cunning glee in the expression, and in many, rather subtle ways we are made aware of something unbalanced in the mentality. The obsessive repetitions 'Maud, Maud, Maud, Maud' and 'Maud is here, here, here' ring through the narrator's mind as the 'crying and calling' of birds. But it is faintly, even here, a madman's fancy; something dark and faintly unwholesome in what sounds like the cawing of rooks, coming from the same mind that later in a still more excited state sees night in the sinister character of the 'black bat'. This is also the section (Part I, 12, 4) that contains that outstanding four-line banality:

> I kiss'd her slender hand,
>   She took the kiss sedately;
> Maud is not seventeen,
>   But she is tall and stately.

It has always seemed incredible that a man of any sense and/or sensibility could have written such a verse, and I am now inclined to think that it, too, is written 'in character'. Taken this way it can have a weird simplicity, as of a simpleton—which the narrator of *Maud* is *not*, except in this mood of light-headed excitement. The key to this section is in the last verse:

> Look, a horse at the door,
>   And little King Charley snarling!
> Go back, my lord, across the moor.
>   You are not her darling.

The 'snarling' here is not only the spaniel's: there is a snarl of over-excited triumph in the tone as the secretive mind records its victory, outsmarting the aristocratic rival. In all this, Tennyson does seem to have achieved some subtlety of characterisation. In such passages, the character becomes a real creation, and no mere mouthpiece for the poet himself.

For Tennyson was by this time, I think, able to look freely at his old self. He had to a very large extent found his way out of the wood by 1850 and the writing of *Maud* completed the dark journey. I think he *had* come near to despair and breakdown at various times during the previous seventeen years. Perhaps the blackest time was after Dr. Allen's scheme came to disaster in 1843. He lost his money and the prospects of marriage. Perhaps his mind went back to that time when he writes in *Maud* (Part I, *1*, 3) of the dead father:

> Did he fling himself down? who knows? for a vast speculation
>   had fail'd,
> And ever he mutter'd and madden'd, and ever wann'd with
>   despair,
> And out he walk'd when the wind like a broken worldling
>   wail'd,
> And the flying gold of the ruin'd woodlands drove thro' the air.

But since then time had been kinder, and now in the middle of life he had enough stability and peace of mind to be able to look at the raptures and despairs of earlier days entering into them again, but now being able to use them for artistic purposes in a way that was closed to him when he had been nearer to them in experience. He was in some measure able to stand aside and create a real character, like himself in part, yet not himself. He could broaden his scope, making 'the madness' a social theme as well as a matter of individual psychology: the madness of the peace that is no peace, where a supposedly Christian society is 'a world of plunder and prey' (Part I, *4*, 4) as surely as is the untamed world of nature where

> The Mayfly is torn by the swallow, the sparrow spear'd by the shrike.

The poem is far stronger for all this. It has marked limitations, admittedly. It fails, I think, to rise to the needs of the climax, for 'Come into the garden, Maud' is brilliant, neat, and exciting in its rhythmic drive, but still not really worthy of its position as the crown and climax to the first 850 lines. Other limitations derive perhaps inevitably from the character of the speaker: the shrillness in denunciation, for example, which weakens the effectiveness of the social criticism. And there is also the radical inadequacy of judgement (whether Tennyson's or the character's) in the idea that through warfare and strong-man government is to come the desperately needed national regeneration. Even so, *Maud* remains one of Tennyson's major achievements; and his own special love for it is easy to understand.

It was written at a period of much happiness in his life. Marriage had not immediately brought freedom from troubles, but now at last things were coming right. Now, for example, they had children; now they had a real home. The first child had been born dead. This was in April 1851, and Alfred wrote about the sad event to John Forster:

> My poor boy died in being born. My wife is safe as yet, but I rather dread the third day. The nurse dressed up the little body in pure white. He was a grand massive manchild, noble brow and hands, which he had clenched in his determination to be born. Had he lived, the doctor said he would have been lusty and healthy, but somehow he got strangled. I kissed his poor pale hands and came away, and they buried him last night in Twickenham churchyard.

Next year, on August 11, all was well, and on March 16, 1854,

Emily gave birth to a second son. Alfred on this occasion was watching the stars and saw Mars culminating in the Lion. He was looking forward to the declaration of war against Russia, and this seemed a doubly significant omen. So they christened the baby Lionel. The first, of course, was named Hallam.

The tragedy of the stillborn baby was probably due to a fall Emily had during her pregnancy. This occurred early in 1851 when the pair were virtually homeless. They had taken a frightful old house near Horsham, where the wind actually blew down a wall of their bedroom, and where a gang of thieves and murderers had their headquarters in the Lodge. They found something better at Twickenham, and then in 1853 came a visit to the Isle of Wight, and the discovery of Farringford.

This was an eighteenth-century house near Freshwater, very beautiful, and, what was vastly important to Tennyson, very secluded. Not that it remained so for long, for the fame of the Poet Laureate and the striking appearance of the man attracted trippers who seem to have gone to all lengths to catch a glimpse of him. Some merely peered over the gate, others came up and pressed their faces to the windows. Some climbed up trees; many helped to pick the summer-house to pieces in their search for souvenirs. One day he was pursued 'full cry along the road by two fat women and sixteen children'. Another time he answered the door to find Americans who said they meant to see Mr. Tennyson. 'Well, now you have seen me, will you kindly go away?' was the reply. Of course, one suspects that he made a bit more of this persecution than he need have done, and that his vanity may have been touched by it in a way he would have been horrified to admit. But it was a genuine flaw in the contentment of the years at Farringford, and was the chief cause of the move in 1867 to his 'solitude' at Aldworth.

Life at Farringford was full of happiness even so. Tennyson was an active man and he enjoyed working on his estate. He made the summer-house, cut new glades in the copses, and went out to sea with the fishermen, reciting his poems to them under the stars and finding them the best audience in the world. Friends came to visit. Benjamin Jowett's friendship dates from this time; that of Edward Lear also. Fitzgerald came in 1854, playing Mozart from an apparently inexhaustible memory, sketching wild flowers and being generally 'delightfully amusing', as Emily's diary has it. Great men played with the children: Kingsley on Guy Fawkes Day in 1856, Jowett at Christmas. That same year also brought the Prince Consort, who talked gaily and took away a bunch of cowslips to make cowslip tea for the Queen. Less celebrated people were also among Tennyson's cherished friends. There was Sir John Simeon, cultivated head of a pleasant neighbouring family, and in 1860 the Camerons arrived. These people had been kind to Tennyson at the time of Hallam's birth, and now they came to raise the temperature of life at Freshwater. 'I hear a trampling in the drive where I am dressing before dinner', wrote Emily in her diary, 'and think it is Americans coming . . . to ask for admittance, but find that it is Mrs. Cameron's grand piano which she has most kindly sent for Mr. Lear.' Julia Cameron's energies and affections would burst forth like buds in springtime, and her enthusiasms were boundless. At one time it would be a recipe, at another a remedy. She even persuaded Tennyson to be vaccinated: 'You're a coward, Alfred, a coward,' she would cry until the poor man gave in. As it happened, the vaccine was bad, and he was laid up with a bad leg for some months after. The camera was another formidable weapon in her armoury, and with it she took a famous photograph (facing page 80) of the poet, strong in the bones and the neck, serious, perhaps even tragic, about the eyes, and marvellously tangled and unkempt about the whiskers. 'The dirty monk' he used to call it.

There was also poetry. Much was written, still more was read aloud after dinner. These readings were great occasions for a visitor; overwhelming as often as not, and people would find themselves saying and really believing that this surely was the greatest poetry in the language. The whole business of hospitality at Farringford, with the Laureate's reading of *Maud* as its climax, has much about it that at this date makes us smile. Sir Harold Nicolson does a brilliantly unkind sketch of it in his *Tennyson* (pp. 170-174). But people did not find the occasions funny at the time; and generally they retained them as vivid memories for many a year afterwards. Lady Ritchie (Thackeray's daughter) has left an account of the poet's readings on these evenings:

> It is a sort of mystical incantation, a chant in which every note rises and falls and reverberates again. As we sit around the twilight room at Farringford, with its great oriel-window looking to the garden, across fields of hyacinths and self-sown daffodils towards the sea, where the waves wash against the rock, we seem carried by a tide not unlike the ocean's sound; it fills the room, it ebbs and flows away; and when we leave, it is with a strange music in our ears, feeling that we have, for the first time, perhaps, heard what we have read a hundred times before.

As for the writings themselves, one might well have expected more 'laureate' poems, more 'howling of patriotic staves', as his friend Franklin Lushington put it, now that Tennyson was an official poet. Oddly, the poem that most fits that description was published anonymously. *Britons, guard your own* appeared in 1852, casting a baleful look towards France where Louis Napoleon had just come to power, and a prophetically hopeful look across the Atlantic: it is to America, this 'gigantic daughter of the West', that Britain might turn 'should war's mad blast again be blown'. In *Hands all round*, written about the same time, he made one of the first of those emotional hymns to the British Empire that became so popular about fifty years later when *Land of Hope and Glory* almost became a second national anthem:

> To all the loyal hearts who long
> To keep our English Empire whole!
> To all our noble sons, the strong
> New England of the Southern Pole!
> To England under Indian skies,
> To those dark millions of her realm!
> To Canada whom we love and prize,
> Whatever statesman hold the helm.

The 'hymn' was in fact a drinking song; and Tennyson found himself in some unexpected trouble with the Temperance

Society to whom he had to explain that when he said 'drink to England' he did not really mean it. He wrote the poem with tears streaming down his cheeks. A third short and patriotic poem, published in *The Times* under his own name, came out in 1859, voicing enthusiasm for the Government's newly proposed Volunteer Force which was to help frighten off the French:

> There is a sound of thunder afar
> Storm in the South that darkens the day!
> Storm of battle and thunder of war!
> Well if it do not roll our way.
> Storm, Storm, Riflemen form!
> Ready, be ready against the storm!
> Riflemen, Riflemen, Riflemen form!

Four hundred War Office clerks answered the call forthwith, and Tennyson himself sent £5. Nor did he forget the Navy:

> The lasses and the little ones, Jack Tars, they look to you!
> The despots over yonder, let 'em do whate'er they please!
> God bless the little isle where a man may still be true!
> God bless the noble isle that is Mistress of the Seas!

The Jack Tars ('my hearties') were never to have the benefit of this, however, for the poem remained unpublished.

A more celebrated piece was *The Charge of the Light Brigade*: 'not a poem on which I pique myself', said Tennyson. In December, 1854, *The Times* gave an account of the famous disaster, and the poem began to take shape round the phrase 'someone had blundered' (it was not surprising, for the Brigade was commanded by Lord Cadogan, 'the Noble Yachtsman', who directed operations from his luxurious private boat in Balaclava Bay). Tennyson dashed the verses off in a few minutes, and they proved a great success with everyone except the other branch of the Tennyson family, where it was pronounced 'horrid rubbish'. The lines are so familiar by this time that it is hard to judge the merits of that critical comment: on the whole I think there might be something in it.

> Cannon to right of them,
> Cannon to left of them,

Cannon in front of them
   Volley'd and thunder'd;
Storm'd at with shot and shell,
Boldly they rode and well,
Into the jaws of Death,
Into the mouth of hell,
   Rode the six hundred.

Whether the lines were good poetry or bad, they were a success with the men in the Crimea: 'Half are singing it and all want to have it in black and white, so as to read what has so taken them', wrote a chaplain from Scutari. It made an unusual appeal to the hunting gentry of the Isle of Wight, too. Sir John Simeon recited it to them as they were waiting for the scent, and Emily Tennyson recorded in her diary that the huntsmen listened intently, 'forgetting why they had come there'.

A 'laureate' poem that deserved more enthusiasm but met with much less was the *Ode on the Death of the Duke of Wellington* (1852). Wellington's death was obviously no time for recalling the fact that he had placed his formidable self in opposition to practically every desirable change since 1815; and of course Tennyson would not have wanted to recall this anyway. Instead, Wellington could be seen as a great man who represented England as she had been in days of former greatness, a sort of emblem of the true standards in national life from which, in the 'fifties, Tennyson felt we were declining.

But wink no more in slothful overtrust.
Remember him who led your hosts;
He bade you guard the sacred coasts.
Your cannons moulder on the seaward wall;
His voice is silent in your council-hall
For ever; and whatever tempests lour
For ever silent; even if they broke
In thunder, silent; yet remember all
He spoke among you, and the Man who spoke;
Who never sold the truth to serve the hour,
Nor palter'd with Eternal God for power;

Who let the turbid streams of rumour flow
Thro' either babbling world of high and low;
Whose life was work, whose language rife
With rugged maxims hewn from life;
Who never spoke against a foe;
Whose eighty winters freeze with one rebuke
All great self-seekers trampling on the right.
Truth-lover was our England's Alfred named;
Truth-lover was our English Duke;
Whatever record leap to light
He never shall be shamed.

The Ode is strong and eloquent. The plain but sonorous style has a certain massive authority, and the solemn, measured rhythm, heavy like a dead march, is also appropriate and impressive. So the first lines:

Bury the Great Duke
With an empire's lamentation

have a boldness of attack, and a rightness of feeling for a great national occasion. The last lines, too, ring with depth and finality:

Speak no more of his renown,
Lay your earthly fancies down,
And in the vast cathedral leave him,
God accept him, Christ receive him!

If Sir Charles Tennyson's judgement that this poem is 'perhaps his greatest' seems to claim too much, it is partly because of the subject-matter; it can tap genuinely deep feeling in Tennyson, yet not the deepest or the most valuable. It is also partly because of the language which is sometimes too much like a versified oration, sometimes too insistent and heavy in its rhyme and metre. The first lines, for example, are splendid, but the fourth line seems unfortunate—clumsy in its movement and banal in the rhyme:

Bury the Great Duke
With an empire's lamentation;

> Let us bury the Great Duke
> To the noise of the mourning of a mighty nation;

One says 'seems' because if the line is read in the emphatic, incantatory manner which was probably Tennyson's own, it comes to be acceptable. But the eye does not readily take to it. Nor does the inner ear (mine at any rate) enjoy being pummelled by the insistent rhymes of the next sections: deplore-roar-wrought for-fought for-evermore, in the first, and slow-woe-go-grow-blow-low in the second. Still, whatever one's criticism of these things, it still seems remarkably damnable of the Victorian public that they found so little merit in the poem when it appeared. 'An intrinsically poor performance', G. H. Lewes (George Eliot's husband) called it in *The Leader*; and Thomas Huxley, the great evolutionist, sent a copy of it to a friend 'by way of packing—it is not worth much more'.

It is often surprising to us to see how much of Tennyson's work was attacked when it appeared. Any notion of him as a sacred patriarchal figure in mid-Victorian England is at best only a quarter-truth. The hostility to *Maud* in 1855 was particularly marked and it disappointed Tennyson bitterly. Sometimes he hit back with unexpected wit, as when a critic wrote: 'If an author pipe of adultery, fornication, murder and suicide, set him down as the practiser of those crimes'. Tennyson replied, 'Adulterer I may be, fornicator I may be, murderer I may be, suicide I am not yet'. But generally he was much hurt by the fury his poem provoked and his great fondness for it no doubt grew in proportion to the criticisms: 'Perhaps why I am sensitive over her (*Maud*) is because she is abused', he said. 'Mothers always make the most of a defective child.'

Still, his fame grew. Honours increased. The year of *Maud*'s publication was also the year of Tennyson's honorary degree at Oxford ('Did your mother call you early, Mr. Tennyson?' was the shout of an undergraduate in the Sheldonian). At about the same time a lake was named after him in New Zealand and a cape in the Arctic. His celebrity menaced him even when he went abroad. Portugal, Spain and North Africa all had their share of autograph hunters. The stream of eminent Victorians calling at Farringford continued, and eventually he was summoned to visit the most eminent of all. When Prince Albert died in 1861, Tennyson wrote the famous lines that eventually were placed as a Preface to the *Idylls of the King*. The *Idylls* ('a sort of Albert Memorial in verse,' F. L. Lucas calls them) were dedicated to the late Consort:

> we see him as he moved,
> How modest, kindly, all-accomplished, wise,
> With what sublime repression of himself,
> And in what limits, and how tenderly;
> Not swaying to this faction or to that;
> Not making his high place the lawless perch
> Of wing'd ambitions, nor a vantage-ground
> For pleasure; but thro' all this tract of years
> Wearing the white flower of a blameless life,
> Before a thousand peering littlenesses,
> In that fierce light which beats upon a throne
> And blackens every blot;

He addressed himself to the Queen in the lines that followed, and she, deeply touched by Tennyson's tribute, received him at Osborne in April the following year. She wrote of the interview in her diary:

> I went down to see Tennyson, who is very peculiar-looking, tall, dark, with a fine head, long black flowing hair, and a beard; oddly dressed, but there is no affectation about him. I told him how much I admired his glorious lines to my precious Albert, and how much comfort I found in his *In Memoriam*. He was full of unbounded appreciation of my beloved Albert. When he spoke of my own loss, of that of the nation, his eyes quite filled with tears.

Meanwhile the composition of the *Idylls* had begun: the Arthurian poems which Tennyson hoped would be the crown of his life's work. In 1856 he started on the first of these, and twenty years later they were complete. 'We know not where to look in history or in letters for a nobler or more overpowering conception of man as he might be,' said Gladstone. 'They swarm with beautiful passages', wrote A. C. Bradley in 1914. 'But the whole, beyond doubt, fails to satisfy.' That balanced judgement is closer than Gladstone's to the verdict of our own age. And, even then, to many it may seem a little too generous.

A NOTE ON 'MAUD' AND 'ALTON LOCKE'

Alton Locke, the hero of Kingsley's novel, is a much more wholesome character than the narrator of *Maud*, but he too is a romantic passionate creature, given to fits of depression, and eventually coming near to madness. He speaks of 'that peculiar melancholy of intellectual youth' with which he was afflicted, and adds 'I battened on my own melancholy'. Like the 'I' of *Maud*, he also 'began to look on man as the creature and puppet of circumstance' (cf. 'We are puppets, Man in his pride', *Maud*, Part I, *4*, *5*). Later he comments: 'the reader may begin to suspect that I was fast going mad; and I believe I was. If he has followed my story with a human heart, he may excuse me of any extreme weakness, if I did at moments totter on the verge of that abyss' (cf. 'My life has crept so long on a broken wing Thro' cells of madness, haunts of horror and fear', *Maud*, Part III, first lines). This man's crisis, we are to take it, has brought him also to the verge of insanity.

Even the form of *Maud* may have been partially suggested by a sentence in *Alton Locke*: 'Then I set to work to write an autobiography—at least to commit to paper in regular order the most striking incidents and conversations which I did recollect, and which I had noted down as they occurred in my diary.' The autobiographical diary-form of *Maud*, unconnected by formal narrative, might be the raw material for such a novel as this. The love story, too, has certain affinities with Tennyson's. Lillian (Tennysonian name) is described as follows: 'Yes, there she was, the foremost among a bevy of girls, "herself the fairest fair", all April smiles and tears, golden curls, snowy rosebuds, and hovering clouds of lace—a fairy queen; but yet—but yet—how shallow that hazel eye, how empty of meaning those delicate features compared with the strength and intellectual richness of the face which had preceded her!' (cf. 'Queen rose of the rosebud garden of girls,' *Maud*, Part I, 22, 9 and the narrator's first impression of Maud with her 'delicate' nose and lack of positive character.)

Readers of *Tennyson's 'Maud', the Biographical Genesis* by R. W. Rader, discussed in this chapter, may recognise other and rather stranger connections between Tennyson and *Alton Locke*. For just as Mr. Rader argues that Tennyson came to see his youthful passion for Rosa Baring as a sensual attraction and therefore harmful, so Alton Locke's devotion to Lillian is seen as a mistake of the undisciplined heart. It is not until late in the novel that we see Lillian clearly as the shallow and sensual flirt that she is. But meanwhile, Alton's infatuation has placed him in many a false position. He compromises his principles partly 'for the sake of popularity, money, patronage', but more particularly because 'all that involved seeing more of Lillian. They were only too powerful inducements in themselves, alas! but I believe I could have resisted them tolerably, if they had not been backed by love.' This kind of 'love' that is really infatuation, a prompting of the flesh, came more and more to be seen by Tennyson as a cause of great evil in the world. In the story of Alton Locke he must have found much that coincided with his own belief and (perhaps) experience. For as Alton came to discover true love in the 'pure' sympathy of another woman, Eleanor, so Tennyson found in Emily Sellwood his ideal of 'pure' love, the sensual passions being subdued by something 'nobler'. In addition to all this, *Alton Locke* contains glowing tributes to 'Mr. Tennyson', so the poet must have found it particularly satisfying reading. The two works, *Alton Locke* and *Maud*, have much in them, of course, that is not common to both, but the affinities are great enough to suggest that the novel made a deep impression on Tennyson. He read it, according to Sir Charles Tennyson, in 1850 and this in turn supports Mr. Rader's belief that *Maud* (published in 1855) was in some way formulating in Tennyson's mind earlier than is usually thought.

8

'Idylls of the King'

'I tried in my "Idylls" to teach men the need of the ideal, but I feel sometimes as if my life had been a very useless one' (Tennyson in 1886)

Long poems are generally more often talked about than read. Everybody knows the right thing to say about *The Faerie Queen* and *Paradise Lost*, but very few carry more than fragments of them about in their heads, and most would confess, if pressed, to a reading of this bit and that with pious hopes of completing the experience sometime later in life. When the *Idylls of the King* come into question, one can press far less hard and obtain a far more unblushing confession. 'Well, I've dipped', people will say, 'but really life's too short for more than a few of them. Besides . . .' And the unfinished sentence will mean that the poetry is poor stuff and that nobody takes it seriously anyway.

For myself, I have found that the 'this-bit-and-that' approach yields little, and that a fairly fast sweep through the whole work is surprisingly enjoyable. 'They swarm with beautiful passages', was Bradley's view, 'but the whole, beyond doubt, fails to satisfy.' Oddly, I think the poem can work in quite the opposite way. It is rare, in my experience, that one wants to pause over any particular passage. The narrative is straightforward; the reading moves at the story-teller's pace. A vivid simile here, the suggestion of a symbol there, a touch of humour that does not come off, a moment of warm 'Victorian' humanity that does: all these are incidental characteristics that one notes, but they do not check one's reading or send one back over a passage to read it more intensively. Very few lines demand or reward the kind of attention one must give to a poem by Yeats or Hopkins. On the other hand, reading the work quickly but as a whole, one becomes aware of design, of themes, cross-references and block-contrasts. Moreover there is, after all, something gigantic and powerful in the sheer span: the rise and fall of a whole civilisation, the creation of a noble way of life, the slow corruption and the eventual disaster. The conception has its magnificence.

Impressive too is Tennyson's devotion to his project. It formed a major part of his life between 1856 and 1876, and the whole operation extended over a longer period still. *Morte d'Arthur*, which he incorporated in the *Idylls* in 1869, was written in its original form about 1833; and *Balin and Balan*, written in 1872, was not published till 1884. For half-a-century, then, the concept of a grand work based on the Arthurian legend grew in Tennyson's mind, becoming clearer in details, in proportion and purposes throughout the whole period. At first it may have been an attraction towards something 'not yet done' in literature. When discussing his policy as a writer in the thirties, he said he felt bound to produce relatively short poems, as 'the big things' had been done—except for King Arthur (in fact Malory, Dryden, William Morris and Matthew Arnold had all 'done' Arthur or Arthurian tales, but there was nothing on the scale or of the high-seriousness which Tennyson proposed). He was reading Sir Thomas Malory's Arthurian tales in the early thirties, and his own poems of those years included *Sir Galahad*, an imaginative, buoyant piece, *Sir Launcelot and Queen Guinevere*, which he called *A Fragment*, and of course *Morte d'Arthur*. With the others, this was published in 1842, prefaced by an interesting passage called *The Epic* and returning to the same material at the end. *The Epic* tells how after a party on Christmas-Eve, four men, friends probably from University days, sat round the fire and persuaded the poet amongst them to dig out one of his old compositions and recite it. He does so and—

with some prelude of disparagement,
Read, mouthing out his hollow oes and aes,
Deep-chested music, and to this result.

'This result' is *Morte d'Arthur*. When it is over the company breaks up, to go to bed and dream of Arthur 'like a modern gentleman Of stateliest port' until awoken as 'The clear church-bells ring in the Christmas morn'. *The Epic* is interesting partly because vivid and (one feels) personal; also because it anticipates and shows some recognition of the force of criticisms which were to be levelled many years later at the *Idylls* themselves. The imagined poet in this group had, apparently, written an Arthurian Epic when at college. It had twelve books, just as the *Idylls* eventually had, and the poet had destroyed all but this one because they were 'faint Homeric echoes', merely literary and archaic, and irrelevant to modern life. Nevertheless, the company 'sat rapt':

> it was the tone with which he read—
> Perhaps some modern touches here and there
> Redeem'd it from the charge of nothingness—
> Or else we loved the man and prized his work.

The Epic suggests that the form which was to become the *Idylls of the King* had been conceived in Tennyson's mind even as early as this, but that he was very hesitant about it and on the whole tended to draw back from it. Even so, it persisted and in 1849 a journal, evidently with some inside information, recorded that 'Tennyson's poem of King Arthur is not yet commenced, though he has been for years past maturing the conception of it, and he intends that it should occupy him for some fifteen years'.

If Tennyson drew back from undertaking an Arthurian epic, it was partly out of a high sense of the demands it would make. As a Shakespearean actor might refuse to play King Lear till he has reached fifty, reckoning that the part demands all possible maturity and experience, so Tennyson reserved himself for what he had long hoped would be his greatest work. But another reason was no doubt the one suggested in *The Epic*: that Arthurian stories were eminently open to the charges of 'nothing-ness' or imitativeness. The critics were constantly urging upon him his duties to society, which to them meant teaching, and preaching too; not merely 'singing' and certainly not singing about a remote age without relevance to the present. It is also clear that even at this stage Tennyson himself believed that such charges would be unjust. *Morte d'Arthur* includes 'some modern touches', and in the famous passage:

> The old order changeth, yielding place to new,
> And God fulfils himself in many ways,
> Lest one good custom should corrupt the world . . .

Tennyson is extending the application of the mediaeval tale, giving it philosophical point, and so showing that, for him, the old story had meaning and use beyond its romance-book origins. The *Sir Launcelot and Queen Guinevere* fragment also contains in embryo the matter which is to be right at the centre of the *Idylls*: a moral concern, and one which Tennyson believed had every relevance to his own times. Lancelot was the chief of Arthur's knights and the most trusted of his friends. He was also in love with the Queen and she with him. The *Fragment* refers to this only in the last verse and then only obliquely:

> As she fled fast thro' sun and shade,
> The happy winds upon her play'd,
> Blowing the ringlet from the braid.
> She look'd so lovely, as she sway'd
> The rein with dainty finger-tips,
> A man had given all other bliss,
> And all his worldly worth for this,
> To waste his whole heart in one kiss
> Upon her perfect lips.

Over the years Tennyson came to see this kind of love more and more unequivocally as an evil. Even in the *Fragment* it is shown to us as a sensual infatuation and as a cause of wastage, but no explicit judgement is passed. This may, after all, be a case of the world well lost for love. But, as time went by, Tennyson became more certain that a passion ruled over by sexual attraction was evil in itself and the cause of untold further evils in both the individual and society. In the *Idylls of the King* we see society in three stages. First, in the state of lawlessness which Arthur comes to reform; then, in the joyful freshness of Arthur's regenerating reign

> When every morning brought a noble chance,
> And every chance brought out a noble knight.

and then in a state of corruption from which the ultimate disaster inevitably derives. By hint and rumour, we gradually become aware of an evil in the place next to the throne; we see it cause a breakdown of respect and authority, giving also example and excuse for others to sacrifice principles to desire; and finally the state has become so compromised from within, so much rotted with cynicism and degeneracy, that it falls to its enemies, and the reign of the Beast begins anew. The worm at the heart of the flower is what we should call sex, or what he saw as the sensual love of one human being for another, a power strong enough to make both of the people involved sacrifice the basic principle of loyalty, and so, ultimately, their own self-respect and happiness and that of the society of which they are part.

The first association of Lancelot and Guinevere occurs in the first of the twelve books, *The Coming of Arthur*:

> Then Arthur charged his warrior whom he loved
> And honor'd most, Sir Lancelot, to ride forth
> And bring the Queen, and watched him from the gates;
> And Lancelot past away among the flowers—
> For then was latter April—and return'd
> Among the flowers, in May, with Guinevere.

The images of springtime mirror the fresh, new life that comes upon the land as Arthur begins his reign. Lancelot, as the flower of chivalry and honour, appears again in the second book, *Gareth and Lynette*, and again all is fresh and untainted. He seconds Gareth in his trials, and is always seen to set the standard of perfect manhood. But in the third book, *The Marriage of Geraint*, we have the first mention of an illicit affair, and see some of its unhappy effects:

> But when a rumour rose about the Queen,
> Touching her guilty love for Lancelot,

> Tho' yet there lived no proof, nor yet was heard
> The world's loud whisper breaking into storm,
> Not less Geraint believ'd it; and there fell
> A horror on him lest his gentle wife,
> Thro' that great tenderness for Guinevere,
> Had suffer'd or should suffer any taint
> In nature.

There follows in this book and the fourth (*Geraint and Enid*) the wretched story of Geraint's decline, his suspicions, his monstrous testing of Enid and the fate to which it brings both of them so close. We are made to see the enervating influence of sensuality both in the picture of the Queen herself:

> So with the morning all the court were gone.
> But Guinevere lay late into the morn,
> Lost in sweet dreams, and dreaming of her love
> For Lancelot, and forgetful of the hunt.

and in the indirect effect this affair of the Queen's has upon Geraint's life:

> He compass'd her [his wife] with sweet observances
> And worship, never leaving her, and grew
> Forgetful of his promise to the King,
> Forgetful of the falcon and the hunt,
> Forgetful of the tilt and tournament,
> Forgetful of his glory and his name,
> Forgetful of his princedom and its cares.

In turn this has its effect upon society:

> And by and by the people, when they met
> In twos and threes, or fuller companies,
> Began to scoff and jeer and babble of him
> As of a prince whose manhood was all gone,
> And molten down in mere uxoriousness.

And so authority is undermined, leadership ceases to set a right example, and society degenerates.

In *Balin and Balan*, the next book, we see another tragedy which has its origins in the affair between Lancelot and the

Queen. Balin, who worships Guinevere, is embittered to the heart when made to believe that the sneers and rumours he has heard are true. In fact the tale told to him is a lie, but the situation is one that plays into the hands of liars. The wicked Vivien tells the simple Balin a tale which is made to sound circumstantial and convincing, and it is more lascivious than anything yet said. But though Vivien has invented this, the lie is still close to the truth. In an earlier section of this Book, Lancelot and Guinevere have met in a garden of roses and lilies. Lancelot implicitly asserts his will to chastity: he talks of a 'maiden Saint who stands with lily in hand', and the lily is used as a symbol of purity. But the Queen opposes this:

> 'Sweeter to me,' she said, 'this garden rose
> Deep-hued and many-folded!'

She is asserting her will to sensual love, and using the rose as a symbol of this. So the lust of the mind is there, which Christ condemned as much as the act of the body. In a more profound sense, then, Vivien's lie gives a report only one degree worse than the truth deserves. Vivien describes shameless adulterers, whereas in fact there is both restraint and shame. But the basic betrayal of loyalty through sensual desire is still real.

The tale of *Merlin and Vivien* follows. This too keeps the affair of Lancelot and Guinevere in sight. Vivien, an evil, ambitious creature, watches them 'get to horse':

> 'Is that the Lancelot? goodly—ay, but gaunt;
> Courteous—amends for gauntness—takes her hand—
> That glance of theirs, but for the street, had been
> A clinging kiss—how hand lingers in hand!
> Let go at last!—they ride away—to hawk
> For waterfowl. Royaller game is mine.
> For such a supersensual sensual bond
> As that gray cricket chirpt of at our hearth—
> Touch flax with flame—a glance will serve—the liars!

Then comes the first prophecy of the destruction which this fault is going to make possible:

Ah little rat that borest in the dyke
Thy hole by night to let the boundless deep
Down upon far-off cities while they dance—
Or dream—of thee they dream'd not—nor of me
These—ay, but each of either; ride and dream
The mortal dream that never yet was mine—
Ride, ride and dream until ye wake—to me!

But the tale also enforces the point by providing a further example of it. Just as sensual passion is the hole which lets in 'the boundless deep' and the ruin of Arthur's kingdom, so the wisest of men, Merlin the magician, finds himself destroyed by desires he cannot quite control. Vivien vamps, teases and cajoles; and the old man—

Tho' doubtful, felt the flattery, and at times
Would flatter his own wish in age for love,
And half believe her true.

But for the power of sensuality over intellect, Merlin would never have had anything to do with the girl. As it is he has opened himself to the practice of her wiles, tells her the secret she desires, and is annihilated:

Then crying, 'I have made his glory mine,'
And shrieking out, 'O fool!' the harlot leapt
Adown the forest, and the thicket closed
Behind her, and the forest echo'd 'fool'.

In *Lancelot and Elaine*, we see, more movingly than elsewhere in the *Idylls*, the personal tragedy of Lancelot, and also the tragedy of the woman who might have been his wife. The scandal has by this time risen from a loud whisper, and a storm is imminent. The affair in the court is now common knowledge in the provinces:

'But this I know, for all the people know it,
He loves the Queen, and in an open shame,
And she returns his love in open shame.'

As a consequence of this, the beautiful and devoted Elaine dies
and Lancelot has lost the woman who might have brought him—

> now a lonely man
> Wifeless and heirless, noble issue, sons
> Born to the glory of thy name and fame,
> My knight, the great Sir Lancelot of the Lake.

So speaks the King, and every word to Lancelot seems a reproach. Shame takes possession of him, for from the start of
this Idyll we have seen him as a man who knows himself to be
in a false position, so that even his creditable actions are somehow spoilt by the basic falseness in his life:

> The shackles of an old love straiten'd him,
> His honour rooted in dishonour stood,
> And faith unfaithful kept him falsely true.

The Holy Grail, Book VIII, brings the disintegration of
Arthur's rule one stage nearer, though it only occasionally has
any reference to the guilty love-affair. *Pelleas and Etarre* brings
it nearer still, for now a cynical and disillusioned sophistication
has come over this once simple, vigorous and virtuous society.
Society now is old in its knowledge of evil. Pelleas is the one
remaining innocent and he is now cruelly undeceived:

> Then fared it with Sir Pelleas as with one
> Who gets a wound in battle, and the sword
> That made it plunges thro' the wound again,
> And pricks it deeper; and he shrank and wail'd,
> 'Is the Queen false?' and Percivale was mute.
> 'Have any of our Round Table held their vows?'
> And Percivale made answer not a word.

Now the twilight of Arthur's reign has really begun, and it is
clear that the final darkness is approaching:

> The Queen
> Look'd hard upon her lover, he on her,
> And each foresaw the dolorous day to be;
> And all talk died, as in a grove all song
> Beneath the shadow of some bird of prey.

> Then a long silence came upon the hall,
> And Modred thought, 'The time is hard at hand!'

And so it is, for, in *The Last Tournament*, civilisation, hard pressed by the barbaric hordes of its enemies outside, is shown to be in the final stages of degeneration within itself. Everything now is second-rate. A poor, style-less and boorish tournament forces the recognition upon everybody:

> And most of these were mute, some anger'd, one
> Murmuring, 'All courtesy is dead', and one,
> 'The glory of our Round Table is no more'.

The Chorus to this part of the drama is the weird figure of a jester, Dagonet, who—

> high above the yellowing woods,
> Danced like a wither'd leaf before the hall.

Such images set the tone throughout:

> The dirty nurse, Experience, in her kind
> Hath foul'd me.

So says the fool, and so might the wise and righteous Arthur. The story of Tristram is told in this Book. The dirty nurse, Experience, is at her work there too, for Tristram and Isolt wallow in their sensuality like pagans, and even here the central evil in the whole sequence of poems is emphasised. Tristram is completely cynical about the Round Table, of which he is a sworn member, and about the King to whom he swore allegiance; and what in the first place sapped his loyalty was this same thing, the scandal at court concerning Lancelot and the Queen. Like a disillusioned believer, he admits the absurdity of his former faith:

> Moreover that weird legend of his [Arthur's] birth,
> With Merlin's mystic babble about his end
> Amazed me; then, his foot was on a stool
> Shaped as a dragon; he seem'd to me no man,
> But Michael trampling Satan; so I sware
> Being amazed. But this went by—The vows!

O, ay—the wholesome madness of an hour—
They served their use, their time; for every knight
Believed himself a greater than himself,
And every follower eyed him as a God;
Till he, being lifted up beyond himself,
Did mightier deeds than elsewise he had done,
And so the realm was made. But then their vows—
First mainly thro' that sullying of our Queen—
Began to gall the knighthood, asking whence
Had Arthur right to bind them to himself?

Moreover the sin of Guinevere can now be offered as a precedent and an excuse for the adultery of Tristram and Isolt themselves:

O my soul, be comforted!
If this be sweet, to sin in leading-strings,
If here be comfort, and if ours be sin,
Crown'd warrant had we for the crowning sin
That made us happy.

At the end of this Book, King Mark, Isolt's husband, discovers his wife with Tristram whom he kills; and King Arthur coming home—

All in a death-dumb autumn-dripping gloom

—has learnt of his own wife's untruthfulness, and faces the last darkening of his reign and life. What remains is the designed emotional climax of *Guinevere* and the rounding off of the whole story in *The Passing of Arthur*.

In *Guinevere*, the King speaks to his fallen wife, in the capacity of judge or perhaps God, and only at the end as husband and lover. He does nothing to extenuate the shame of her position, but only makes explicit and still more painful the consequences of her deception.

For thou hast spoilt the purpose of my life

is one plain and painful sentence. This implies not merely the tragedy of an individual but of a nation, for the purpose of Arthur's life was the good of the nation and his fight to fulfil it was already a battle against heavy odds.

Well is it that no child is born of thee.
The children born of thee are sword and fire,
Red ruin, and the breaking up of laws.

'The Beast' reigned till Arthur's coming, and at his passing
come confusion, bloodshed and barbarism. Arthur, speaking to
his Queen, traces the steps by which this has happened, and
Tennyson, in an address to his own Queen at the end of the
whole work, names the forces active in this society which might
work together to bring it to a similar disaster:

Waverings of every vane with every wind,
And wordy trucklings to the transient hour,
And fierce or careless looseners of the faith,
And Softness breeding scorn of simple life,
Or Cowardice, the child of lust for gold,
Or Labour, with a groan and not a voice,
Or Art with poisonous honey stol'n from France,
And that which knows, but careful for itself,
And that which knows not, ruling that which knows
To its own harm.

The poem, he says, is an 'old, imperfect tale', but 'new-old':
that is, the poet means it to apply to the modern Britain, which
he prays may not become 'some third-rate isle'. His tale, he
hopes, has shown 'ideal manhood closed in real man', and it has
also, like the Moralities of old, shown 'Sense at war with Soul'.
He means sexuality at war with Christian principle. He hopes to
have made individuals look at themselves and so to turn the eyes
of a whole society in upon itself, to think what it is and what it
might be. He was very largely doing what his critics had always
wanted him to do; and if fervour and fluency, grandeur of
design and meticulous attention to detail had been enough, he
would have succeeded.

Unfortunately the fervour is too often felt only as enthusiasm
for the moral idea. Only occasionally does the verse catch fire;
all too often it is pale and tired, pedestrian. In *The Coming of
Arthur*, for example, the lines move dully from one statement to
the next. The blank verse is technically flexible enough, with a

high proportion of run-on lines, but the freedom gains little in expressiveness. Where the style achieves strength and character, even then there seems something second-rate about the context so that it registers as not much more than a successful rhetorical device.

> Clang battle-axe, and clash brand! Let the King reign!

catches the percussive effect of drums and cymbals, but the great ceremony that it belongs to is still like a conventional story-book illustration; one never believes that this is reality. The episode has its due place in the whole tale; symbolically it is right. But the style of description with its meticulous detail asks one to accept it as reality, and this is a condition to which it never attains.

The uneasy mixture of old-world speech with Victorian manners and tastes also detracts. The language is often impossible. A fair sample is this speech of Gareth's:

> Old master, reverence thine own beard
> That looks as white as utter truth, and seems
> Wellnigh as long as thou art statured tall!
> Why mockest thou the stranger that hath been
> To thee fair-spoken?

The 'thee's' and 'thine's', the inversion ('been to thee fair-spoken') are bad enough, but nothing to the stiff and pompous archaisms of:

> Wellnigh as long as thou art statured tall!

What is worse, one suspects that we are to take this as a hearty, wholesome kind of humour. The humour throughout is ponderously conscientious at best, and as tedious as possible in the pert speeches of Lynette or the garrulity of Enid's mother:

> And yester-eve I would not tell you of it
> But kept it as a sweet surprise at morn.
> Yea, truly is it not a sweet surprise?

What Robert Louis Stevenson called 'tushery' ('yester-eve', 'Yea, truly'), along with a bumpily syllabic literary-colloquial kind of utterance such as never passed human lips; these are characteristic of the diction in much else besides this particular speech. The elements rarely mix, but remain like floating lumps in the whole substance: recognisably a lump of would-be mediaeval alongside a lump of the purest Victorian. So, for instance, in *The Passing of Arthur* (or *Morte d'Arthur*) we have all the mediaeval wardrobe and scenery—the 'armed heels', the 'white samite, mystic, wonderful', the 'brand Excalibur'— stage-properties, all of them, in a drama that is essentially Victorian.

> So saying, from the pavement he half rose,
> Slowly, with pain, reclining on his arm,
> And looking wistfully with wide blue eyes
> As in a picture.

Exactly 'as in a picture'; a very Victorian picture too.

Nor does it seem likely that we shall ever again feel the emotion of the *Idylls* as Tennyson and his contemporaries could. When he read *Guinevere* aloud, Tennyson's voice would break with emotion, Emily would weep and the visitor would find tears upon his own cheeks also. Edward Lear wrote to Holman Hunt, 'I have read the *Guinevere* which is an absolutely perfect poem—and made me blubber, bottlesfull'. I doubt if anybody has 'blubbered' over it for many a year now, though there are passages in other Idylls (*Lancelot and Elaine, Pelleas and Etarre* especially) which are still moving.

Against some of the criticisms made in Tennyson's own time, one might defend the *Idylls*. Ruskin, speaking of them with great respect, nevertheless implied that he thought them irrelevant to the present:

> . . . it seems to me that so great a power ought not to be spent on visions of things past, but on the living present . . . This seems to me the true task of the modern poet. And I think I have seen faces and heard voices by road and streetside, which claimed or confessed as much as even the loveliest or saddest of Camelot.

But though Tennyson's tales were of the past, he meant them to apply to the present. He meant to show to modern society, first an ideal that should inspire it with a renewed standard of excellence, second a warning and an example of how insidiously corruption can take hold and bring all to ruin. I do not know of much evidence to suggest that Tennyson succeeded in impressing his contemporaries in the ways he wished to. But if he did not, the fault would seem to lie in their reading rather than his writing, for the ideal and its corruption are both solidly *there* in the *Idylls*. It seems that the poems were read in the nineteenth century very largely for their emotional effect, for individual beauties and for the conventionally 'pure' morality. But the whole work is really much more impressive as one follows through from one Idyll to the next the portrait of a changing society: the loss of innocence, virtue and energy, the causes and the effects. This, too, is rendered in the poetry by the changing images: at first of springtime, then of the yellow withering leaf, winter and night, and eventually that 'death-white mist' in which the 'last dim, weird battle' is fought, symbol of the final triumph of confusion in all things, moral uncertainty, political disorder, social lawlessness. In all this the *Idylls of the King* have a certain greatness. In so many other ways, impatience with them is readily understandable.

Sketch of Tennyson made by James Spedding at Mirehouse in April 1835

9

Old Age and Aldworth

'. . . distinctly and emphatically one of the
immortals' ('The Times')

An agreeable romantic notion about the poet is that he is a
passionate man who flames out his thoughts for a brief, ardent
time, then, loved by the gods, dies young. The nineteenth
century had begun with poets who were evidently loved much
too well: Keats, Shelley and Byron all fit the romantic formula.
Even Wordsworth and Coleridge, in a different sense, conform
to the pattern, for their poetic life was soon played out. But the
Victorians themselves were more hardy or more fortunate.
Tennyson lived to a ripe old age, and wrote on and on and on.
He saw most of his great contemporaries to their graves, literally
or figuratively (his presence at Dickens' funeral caused such a
sensation that he was virtually imprisoned in Westminster
Abbey till the authorities rescued him). Nothing is more impressive about the remarkable man than the energy of his old
age. He continued to write to the end of his life, started to
compose for the stage at sixty-five, strode vigorously over
England and Europe in his seventies, and at eighty-one waltzed
'for quite a long time', Sir Charles Tennyson tells us, 'with May
Hichens in the ballroom'. A penalty of all this was that he became an institution, something for the conventional and respectable to revere, and for the young and independent to react
against. 'Talking it over, we agreed that Blake was no good
because he learnt Italian at sixty in order to study Dante, and
we knew Dante was no good because he was fond of Virgil, and
Virgil was no good because Tennyson ran him, and as for

Tennyson—well, Tennyson goes without saying.' So wrote Samuel Butler, speaking for the bright young men of his time, and (as in most things) still more for the bright young men after his time. If Tennyson had died in 1850, he would not have 'gone without saying' quite so readily. He would not have filled the romantic bill, but he would also not have become the monument to Victorianism which he came to seem. And posterity would have lost some remarkable writing.

The poems of the last decades generally possess a strength that the *Idylls* lack. This is not, as it were, a biographical matter. It is not that Tennyson regained in his last twenty years a vigour that he had lost in late middle age, for the poems and the *Idylls* overlap. But turning from one to the other, one feels a far freer poetic life. Perhaps it was that Tennyson was too consciously and weightily impressed by the lofty seriousness of his self-appointed task in the *Idylls*. At any rate, that colossal enterprise did not drain the poetic life out of him, and among these later poems are many of his most interesting, perhaps two or three of his best.

Of these, I think *Aylmer's Field* is one. This is an astonishing poem, written in acid, immensely vigorous in its movement and vocabulary, and touching again a subject very close to Tennyson's heart. Like *Maud* and *Locksley Hall*, it tells of lovers kept apart by family pride, but it bites more effectively than these because the strain of high-pitched, self-pitying complaint is absent. The narrative is supposedly derived from 'a grizzled cripple', but it is not told in the first person and it gains in objectivity from this. He says that the cripple gave the story 'in rougher shape', but one of the exciting things about it is a sense of unchecked spontaneity, an energy that drives the pen forward —something never remotely felt in the *Idylls*:

> Sir Aylmer Aylmer, that almighty man,
> The county God—in whose capacious hall,
> Hung with a hundred shields, the family tree
> Sprang from the midriff of a prostrate king—
> Whose blazing wyvern weathercock'd the spire,
> Stood from his walls and wing'd his entry-gates,

And swang besides on many a windy sign—
Whose eyes from under a pyramidal head
Saw from his windows nothing save his own—
What lovelier of his own had he than her,
His only child, his Edith, whom he loved
As heiress and not heir regretfully?
But 'he that marries her marries her name'.
This fiat somewhat soothed himself and wife,
His wife a faded beauty of the Baths,
Insipid as the queen upon a card;
Her all of thought and bearing hardly more
Than his own shadow in a sickly sun.

Then marvellously the tone changes, modulating through the image of the 'sickly sun', as we look at the village:

A land of hops and poppy-mingled corn,
Little about it stirring save a brook!
A sleepy land, where under the same wheel
The same old rut would deepen year by year;

The conflicting emotions of tenderness and scorn play off against each other to produce verse which is always yielding some boldness of usage or image. Leolin's 'boyish histories', for example, the stories he makes up, are:

sketches rude and faint,
But where a passion yet unborn perhaps
Lay hidden as the music of the moon
Sleeps in the plain eggs of the nightingale.

The jewels on the 'rich sheath' of a dagger are:

Sprinkled about in gold that branch'd itself
Fine as ice-ferns on January panes
Made by a breath.

Into the denunciations came something of that formidable downrightness that we meet in the later pages of Tennyson's biographies:

These old pheasant-lords,
These partridge-breeders of a thousand years,

Who had mildew'd in their thousands, doing nothing
Since Egbert—why, the greater their disgrace!

It is the theme of *Lady Clara Vere de Vere*, written thirty years
or so earlier, with its famous piece of finger-wagging morality:

Kind hearts are more than coronets,
And simple faith than Norman blood.

In *Aylmer's Field* there is less need to be heavily didactic, and the
only major limitation to its success (apart from a shameless bit of
Victorian prettiness about 'tender pink five-beaded baby soles')
occurs when this is forgotten. In the last part of the poem, the
parson is given free rein, and a long sermon is transcribed,
powerful and eloquent, but only making over-explicit and over-
emphatic the moral of the tale. Yet even here there is an energy
of language that commands attention:

Long o'er his bent brows linger'd Averill,
His face magnetic to the hand from which
Livid he pluck'd it forth, and labor'd thro'
His brief prayer-prelude, gave the verse, 'Behold,
Your house is left unto you desolate!'
But lapsed into so long a pause again
As half amazed, half frighted, all his flock;
Then from his height and loneliness of grief
Bore down in flood, and dash'd his angry heart
Against the desolations of the world.

Always in this poem we find that what might have been expressed
in generalities is rendered in an image, specific and imaginative.
The last lines are representative:

Then the great Hall was wholly broken down,
And the broad woodland parcell'd into farms;
And where the two contriv'd their daughter's good,
Lies the hawk's cast, the mole has made his run,
The hedgehog underneath the plantain bores,
The rabbit fondles his own harmless face,
The slow-worm creeps, and the thin weasel there
Follows the mouse, and all is open field.

This has all the strength of a major poet working creatively and in his full maturity.

Not as much can be said for *Enoch Arden*, which was written about the same time and enjoyed a much greater fame. In its way it still stands as a nineteenth-century classic, but that is not entirely to its credit. Too unrestrainedly tear-jerking,* it tells of a fisherman's affections, sufferings, courage, hope and self-sacrifice. Two criticisms are commonly brought against it, both with some justice. One involves a fault of style. The language should be, and usually is, simple and biblical. But occasionally a more grandiose touch, Miltonic and literary, intervenes. This may be Tennyson's way of affirming to his comfortable readers the dignity and nobility of the lower-class story he is telling. 'I am now about my "Fisherman"', he wrote to the Duke of Argyll, 'which is heroic too in its way.' A more troublesome and pervasive weakness, I think, is the Victorianism that cannot resist a touch of warm, intimate prettiness; that will always bring the sad, plucky face, the swimming eyes, before us, never underplaying an emotional situation, always seeming to welcome the opportunity for indulging, like one of its characters, in the fast flow of 'easy tears'. Even so, the poem is still capable of moving one quite deeply, for the tragedy of a man shut out from home and happiness is genuinely felt and vividly rendered by its author, and the situation is itself inherently tragic. Moreover, many imaginative passages compel the reader to enter into Enoch's experiences. In his tropical island where the blaze of the sun is so unremitting, Enoch finds 'a phantom made of many phantoms' which haunts him, memories of:

> people, things, and places, known
> Far in a darker isle beyond the line;
> The babes, their babble, Annie, the small house,
> The climbing street, the mill, the leafy lanes,
> The peacock yew-tree and the lonely Hall,

---

* It is interesting that *Enoch Arden* was suggested to Puccini as a subject for a new opera (see *Puccini among Friends* by Seligman). He liked it but couldn't see it as a stage piece.

> The horse he drove, the boat he sold, the chill
> November dawns and dewy-glooming downs,
> The gentle shower, the smell of dying leaves,
> And the low moan of leaden-colour'd seas.

All this is well caught, and expressed in lines that move with the rare poise that a fully practised poet can command. Even so *Enoch Arden* is only a partial survivor, a hundred years after it was given to an enthusiastic world. The general enthusiasm is not surprising, though it is rather odd to find Matthew Arnold sharing it—and Matthew Arnold, who sternly insisted on the need for intellectual strength in a modern poet, considered this the best of Tennyson's works. Nowadays it registers largely as a period piece, something very central to nineteenth-century taste, kindly, warm, picturesque, moral; unsophisticated, unaristo-cratic, unintellectual, uninvigorating.

This is still more true of *Sea Dreams* and *The Grandmother*, both sentimental pieces celebrated in their time and uncongenial to ours. The former contains the flattest of blank verse lines:

> He suddenly dropt dead of heart-disease.

and the doziest of lullabies:

> What does little birdie say
> In her nest at peep of day?
> Let me fly, says little birdie,
> Mother, let me fly away.

The Grandmother is one of those poems of which it is recorded that the poet 'broke down' while reading it. It has vividness and warmth, and Sir Charles Tennyson calls it a triumph. But the picture of old age is still too sweet to be true. The old lady's mind is a little cloudy but that only adds to the sweetness. None of the less endearing features of old age are present, and the undisturbed muggy warmth of the piece is only emphasised by its heavily sing-song rhythm:

> And Willy's wife has written, she never was over-wise.
> Get me my glasses, Annie; thank God that I keep my eyes.

There is but a trifle left you, when I shall have past away.
But stay with the old woman now; you cannot have long to stay.

Many of the poems written in this and the later period are dramatic monologues, none of them as subtle or as complete creations as the best of Browning's, but interesting and strong all the same. Generally one feels that the character is presented more for the kind of thought and feeling it can express than for interest in its own individuality. As the years went by, Tennyson allowed his pessimistic side more scope than he had formerly done, and the dramatic monologues served again to allow things to be said that could never be presented as the author's own opinions; and indeed they were *not* 'his own opinions' in any simple-minded way. Only they *were* ideas that were part of his brain, notions that troubled him and that he could probably fight best by expressing freely in his poetry. *Despair* (1881) provides an example. This is prefaced by a note: 'A man and his wife having lost faith in a God, and hope of a life to come, and being utterly miserable in this, resolve to end themselves by drowning. The woman is drowned, but the man rescued by a minister of the sect he had abandoned.' The unhappy survivor speaks, cursing the minister for saving him, and expressing his conviction that life and the universe are meaningless:

> Why should we bear with an hour of torture, a moment of pain,
> If every man die for ever, if all his griefs are in vain,
> And the homeless planet at length will be wheel'd thro' the silence of space,
> Motherless evermore of an ever-vanishing race,
> When the worm shall have writhed its last, and its last brother-worm will have fled
> From the dead fossil skull that is left in the rocks of an earth that is dead?

These are not Tennyson's own beliefs, though as usual he found plenty of people who read the poem and assumed that they were. They probably do, however, represent one part or voice in the dialogue that was always going on in his mind: a perpetual exchange between faith and its difficulties, between acceptance of St. Paul's 'all things work together for good to them that love God' and an unhappy knowledge that this was very far from evident in so many human affairs. It is the old debate of *The Two Voices*.

The Ancient Sage (1885 volume) continues it. Two philosophies clash here. One, voiced in short lyrics of great beauty, expresses scepticism about anything beyond this life, and so urges, Omar Khayyam-like, that we should lighten the long darkness of time with the enjoyment our senses make possible:

> Yet wine and laughter, friends! and set
>   The lamps alight, and call
> For golden music, and forget
>   The darkness of the pall.

The Sage, by contrast, sees life as meaningful and good:

> Cleave to the sunnier side of doubt

he urges. And as for the problems and principles of living, he enunciates something similar to Schweitzer's 'reverence for life':

> Nor harm an adder thro' the lust for harm,
> Nor make a snail's horn shrink for wantonness.

Furthermore:

>   curb the beast would cast thee in the mire,
> And leave the hot swamp of voluptuousness,
> A cloud between the Nameless and thyself,
> And lay thine uphill shoulder to the wheel.

This is fundamental Tennysonian doctrine. We have heard it before, but perhaps not so strongly and plainly expressed. Flesh is evil, it says, and very powerful. Fight and overcome it or it will reduce you to the level of the brute creation. The twentieth century has moved further and further from this position. It has urged an unashamed acceptance that sexual needs are part of human nature, and from that point on has debated what freedoms and restrictions the instinct is to move within. Tennyson's standpoint is one of uncompromising suppression, and an apparently growing hatred for the body itself as a distasteful necessity.

In some of the last poems one feels that Tennyson is voicing a disgust with the human race similar to that expressed by Swift in *Gulliver's Travels*. There is that strange dramatic monologue called *Happy*, with its sub-title *The Leper's Bride*. Here the body is:

> This house with all its hateful needs no cleaner than the beast.

It is a 'little city of sewers', and a 'wall of solid flesh' that comes between souls. With it goes a fierce pessimism about the future. In *Locksley Hall Sixty Years After*, the speaker (not necessarily representing Tennyson but surely doing so in large measure) foresees disintegration and chaos in world affairs and in this country's future. And, he says, the writers will have hastened decay. 'Down with Reticence, down with Reverence', seems to be their cry:

> Authors—essayist, atheist, novelist, realist, rhymester, play your part,
> Paint the moral shame of nature with the living hues of art.

> Rip your brothers' vices open, strip your own foul passions bare;
> Down with Reticence, down with Reverence—forward—naked let them stare.

> Feed the budding rose of boyhood with the drainage of your sewer;
> Send the drain into the fountain, lest the stream should issue pure.

> Set the maiden fancies wallowing in the troughs of Zolaism,—
> Forward, forward, ay, and backward, downward too into the abysm!

> Do your best to charm the worst, to lower the rising race of men;
> Have we risen from out the beast, then back into the beast again?

He was observing a very real phenomenon: the easing of Victorian restrictions, the beginnings of psychological investigations into the dark places of men's minds. On the whole the twentieth century has regarded this as progress. Tennyson sees it as change for the worse, and *Locksley Hall Sixty Years After* specifically repudiates the notion that as we go forward 'down the ringing grooves of time' it is to a better civilisation:

> 'Forward' rang the voices then, and of the many mine was one
> Let us hush this cry of 'Forward' till ten thousand years have gone.

As social analysis, there is much that is crude and over-simple, over-rhetorical too, but I personally do not find it laughable or fundamentally wrong-headed. He was, I think, sensing the enormous increase in the speed of change, and the vast strains put upon a civilisation in absorbing beneficial change, let alone in recognising and rejecting what was harmful. Yeats's sense of an impending horror, the feeling that 'the centre cannot hold', is not far off. Nor is Hardy's dismayed view of 'our prematurely afflicted century', as he described it in the Apology of 1922. Tennyson too makes his 'apology'. No doubt, says his speaker, I shall be called reactionary and narrow:

> Cries of unprogressive dotage ere the dotard fall asleep?
> Noises of a current narrowing, not the music of a deep?

Perhaps as we read him now, from a relatively advanced point in our still further afflicted century, we can feel that his passionate warning to us from the nineteenth was not so badly aimed.

This poem was published in 1886. Three years later came the last volume to appear in his lifetime, *Demeter and Other Poems*; a further volume, including *The Death of Oenone*, was published posthumously in 1892. This output is remarkable enough, but it represents only a part of Tennyson's work during these last decades, for between 1865 and his death he also wrote three rather more-than-full-length tragedies, and three shorter plays as well.

He became drawn to the theatre partly through the new life brought into it by Henry Irving. Irving, then a young man, acted Hamlet in a way that was not all sound and fury and that signified a great deal more than usual. Shakespeare was no longer box-office death, and so drama that was Shakespearean could be tried. New techniques of production, principally an ever-more elaborate, eye-charming realism, drew a large public to the theatre, and it was at the Lyceum* that these wonders were most impressively offered.

'A bold step in the wrong direction' is one critic's view of Tennyson's entry into the theatre (P. F. Baum in *Tennyson Sixty Years After*). Certainly, when seen at worst, his play-writing is bad enough to be funny. *The Cup* (1880) serves for sampling. It opens with the clumsiest of fact-giving soliloquies, including:

> I never felt such passion for a woman
> > (*Brings out a cup and scroll from under his cloak*)
> What have I written to her?
> > (*Reading the scroll*)
> To the admired Camma, wife of Sinnatus the Tetrarch . . .

The characters mouth their asides at length:

> > That I
> With all my range of women should yet shun
> To meet her face to face at once!

Then, when the time comes for action, just as the vile seducer is about to make life difficult for the virtuous wife:

> *Enter Sinnatus* (*seizes him from behind by the throat*)
> SYNORIX (*throttled and scarce audible*): Rome! Rome!
> SINNATUS: Adulterous dog!
> SYNORIX (*stabbing him with Camma's dagger*): What! will you have it?
> (*Camma utters a cry and runs to Sinnatus*)
> SINNATUS (*falls backward*) I have it in my heart—to the Temple —fly—

---

* The Lyceum has taken a tumble along with most things grandly Victorian: it is the pillared and porticoed palais-de-danse left of the Strand opposite Waterloo Bridge.

But Browning liked it, Irving was 'in a great state of enthusiasm and excitement' over it, and the play ran for more than a hundred and thirty performances.

It is always pleasing to have our prejudices confirmed, and no doubt before we even opened the pages we knew that this was the sort of thing Tennyson's plays would turn out to be. The 'major' tragedies, however, are a different matter. *Queen Mary* (1875), *Harold* (1876) and *Becket* (1879) were designed as a trilogy to portray 'the making of England'. Tennyson undertook the subjects partly as he did the *Idylls*, wanting to reach a public whom he could impress with a sense of national inheritance and of their duty to uphold in greatness a country that had known such struggles in the times of its making.

One of his themes is the freeing of England from Roman Catholicism, though it is treated more as a matter of nationalism than of religion. Tennyson meant this, like everything else he wrote, to have relevance in people's minds to their own times, when Rome was again exercising an increasing pull on the allegiance of many influential men. Again, as with the *Idylls*, Tennyson miscalculated. Chronicle plays with characters who begin their sentences 'I had leifer' or who exclaim 'Ha! What! eh?' were unlikely to impress a public with their modernity.

Even so, there are many things about these plays that are admirable. *Queen Mary*, the first of them, does not quite add up to a successful dramatic whole. The construction is too episodic; too often it is as though we watch the pageant go by without sufficient involvement in the individuals. Yet the separate scenes are good. The language, in spite of its half-archaic character, has benefited from the Shakespearean influence upon it. While the *Idylls* had the tiredness of second-hand and often second-rate Milton, the plays have the vigour of second-hand good Elizabethan. 'Fray'd i' the knees, and out at elbow, and bald o' the back, and bursten at the toes' is the Third Citizen's description of a character in the first scene. Later in the play the Queen describes Lord-Chancellor Gardner in these words:

> his big baldness,
> That irritable forelock which he rubs,
> His buzzard beak and deep incavern'd eyes.

Lord Paget describes the bearing of Cranmer after his trial as that of a soldier who:

> Hurls his soil'd life against the pikes and dies.

Perhaps it is true that the merit of Tennyson's writing lies more in descriptive power than in anything peculiarly dramatic. But these characters—Wyatt, Cranmer, Philip, Elizabeth, Mary herself—do have a real existence, and by and large their emotions are imaginatively captured. Mary's own character, its purposefulness and sincerity tragically distorted by an uncontrolled, obsessive love and false beliefs, is presented without simplification; and her suffering is done without sentimentality. Both respectable achievements.

These plays meant hard work for Tennyson. The actual writing was no great struggle—he seems in fact to have composed quite fluently—but his research was always conscientiously done, he read widely, and thought for himself. This, along with a full social programme, was all part of the period in life which for most men means a little gardening, a pipe and a pair of slippers.

He was often thought of by friends in earlier years as being exactly the kind of man who might take to lotos-eating in premature retirement. 'A fine, large-featured, dim-eyed, bronze-coloured, shaggy-headed man is Alfred; dusty, smoky, free and easy, who swims outwardly and inwardly with great composure in an inarticulate element of tranquil chaos and tobacco smoke. Great now and then when he does emerge—a most restful, brotherly, solid-hearted man.' Thus Carlyle in 1840. Half-a-century later the restful man, tranquil, free and easy, was still working. There were many rewards, of course, the most spectacular being the peerage which he accepted in 1883. It brought some criticisms, and there were probably conversations all over the country like the one Yeats's father had with his landlord:

'Do you think now that Tennyson should have been given that peerage?' 'One's only doubt is if he should have accepted it: it was a finer thing to be Alfred Tennyson.' There was a silence, and then: 'Well, all the people I know think he should not have got it.' Then, spitefully: 'What's the good of poetry?' 'O, it gives our minds a great deal of pleasure.' 'But wouldn't it have given your mind more pleasure if he had written an improving book?' 'O, in that case I should not have read it.'

AUTOBIOGRAPHIES, p. 84.

Tennyson had several times refused honours offered to him, but he now saw the peerage as conferring an honour upon literature as well as himself and was proud to take his seat in 'the greatest Upper Chamber in the world'. These last years, however, were not without their troubles. Among the minor ones was the perpetual annoyance of tourists: the move in 1868 to Aldworth, the house built for Tennyson near Haslemere, had been made partly to gain protection from the visitors who had come in droves to the Isle of Wight, but it did not completely succeed. There was a major tragedy in the death of the second son, Lionel, who caught jungle fever in Assam and died on board ship bound for home in 1886. Work was then a blessing. Tennyson kept hard at his *Locksley Hall Sixty Years After*, 'to keep himself up', as Hallam tells us. His own death too was sometimes in his thoughts, and in 1889 he wrote *Crossing the Bar*, the central image coming into his mind on one of the last crossings to Freshwater:

> Sunset and evening star,
>   And one clear call for me!
> And may there be no moaning of the bar,
>   When I put out to sea,
>
>
> But such a tide as moving seems asleep,
>   Too full for sound and foam,
> When that which drew from out the boundless deep
>   Turns again home.

> Twilight and evening bell,
>   And after that the dark!
> And may there be no sadness of farewell,
>   When I embark;
>
> For tho' from out our bourne of Time and Place
>   The flood may bear me far,
> I hope to see my Pilot face to face
>   When I have crost the bar.

'Mind you put *Crossing the Bar* at the end of all editions of my poems', he said to his son some days before he died.

Death came in the grand style. Dr. George Dabbs described the event for readers of *The Times*:

> Nothing could have been more striking than the scene during the last few hours. On the bed a figure of breathing marble, flooded and bathed in the light of the full moon streaming through the oriel window; his hand clasping the Shakespeare which he had asked for but recently, and which he kept by him to the end; the moonlight; the majestic figure as he lay there 'drawing thicker breath', irresistibly brought to one's mind his own *Passing of Arthur*. His last conscious words were words of love addressed to his wife and son—words too sacred to be written here.

The other doctor, Andrew Clark, said it was 'the most glorious [death] he had ever seen', and the Queen appreciated it too:

> Everything must have been most touching and beautiful, and worthy of what the great poet was; the 'passing away' with Shakespeare in his hand, the *very* simple and affecting departure from his own beloved home, and the last sad ceremony when the mortal part of this great man was laid in its final resting-place.

His funeral in Westminster Abbey was, if anything, almost too glorious. 'The great accumulations of flowers', we read, 'made the very air of Poet's Corner faint with too much sweetness.' Among them were wreaths from the Queen and Gladstone. Among the pall-bearers were the Master of Balliol, a United States Minister, and six lords. Among the congregation were

Swinburne, Irving, Huxley, Stanford, Sullivan, Millais, Holman Hunt, Conan Doyle, Coventry Patmore and Thomas Hardy. Dr. Bridge's setting of *Crossing the Bar* was one anthem; Lady Tennyson's own music for *The Silent Voices* was the other. Hall Caine, however, writing in *The Times* a few days later, found the funeral 'not in the truest sense as profoundly impressive . . . as we had hoped it would be'. There was, apparently, 'little to bring tears to the eyes and the throb to the throat'. As moving a sight as any perhaps would have been the 'many' who, according to Hallam Tennyson, 'were seen reading *In Memoriam* while waiting for the service'. Perhaps it was more moving still at Freshwater, where the shops were closed and the blinds drawn.

It is 'the national belief', said *The Times*, 'that the late Lord Tennyson is distinctly and emphatically one of the immortals'. Evidently Tennyson had raised the national status of the poet's art and of his particular appointment, for on the previous occasion of the Laureate's death, *The Times* had declared that the office was unnecessary and should be abolished. The dead Laureate then was Wordsworth. Wordsworth's death was hardly noticed: Tennyson's was a great event. 'English to the back-bone,' said *The Times* first leader, singling out for especial praise his 'serene self-restraint' and the 'fastidious refinement of his taste'. Even *Punch* gave up its large illustration page to an engraving of the poet standing up firmly in a boat yet still looking spirit-like, crowned with laurels and inevitably 'Crossing the Bar'. It also published some pious verses, then in the next numbers sat back gleefully to watch the poets scramble for office. Alfred Austin won.

10

Conclusion

'He is the very Janus of poets. He wears everywhere two faces, and you have scarce begun to admire the one ere you despise the other' (Dryden on Shakespeare)

Dryden stood from Shakespeare at about the distance we stand from Tennyson. He recognised an exceptional poetic force ('He was the man who of all the modern and perhaps ancient poets had the largest soul'), but he belonged to his own age and was irritated when Shakespeare appeared constantly to flout the decorum and moderate good sense which he so valued. We seem to have reached something like this stage with Tennyson. There is general acknowledgement of an eminence: he was an important voice of his age, did write remarkable and fine poems, does survive as a poet with a distinctive voice of his own. We also continue to shy away from him, or from most of him, and we are genuinely appalled or simply derisive when *Airy, fairy Lilian* and *The May Queen* come into view. The face we despise in this Janus of poets is sentimental, prissily pretty and heavily moralistic by turns, softly dreamy or noisily patriotic, earnestly muddled, or just dull. And he *is* all these things. The sentimentalist invites us to blubber bottlesfull (Edward Lear's phrase) over his dying May Queen. All the tricks of deliberately incited emotionalism are there, the sugary *vox humana* and tremolo stops of the sentimentalist's organ:

> Goodnight, goodnight, when I have said goodnight for evermore,
> And you see me carried out from the threshold of the door,
> Don't let Effie come to see me till my grave be growing green.
> She'll be a better child to you than ever I have been.

She'll find my garden-tools upon the granary floor.
Let her take 'em, they are hers; I shall never garden more;
But tell her, when I'm gone, to train the rosebush that I set
About the parlour-window and the box of mignonette.

Another irritant is the prim, curate-like tone of his words to young women (*Maud*, Part I, *20*, *1*):

If one should ask me whether
The habit, hat and feather,
Or the frock and gipsy bonnet
Be the neater and completer;
For nothing can be sweeter
Than maiden Maud in either.

Nor will it do to say that this is the Narrator and not Tennyson speaking, for his early album-pieces to 'Adeline', 'Rosalind' and so forth, are in much the same vein: that of a man looking for some pretty creature to put in his doll's house. His attitude to women is normally better than this. *The Princess*, though it can hardly be said to fight the good fight, not hard enough, at any rate, to worry the enemy much, does argue for the respect due to women as thinking creatures; and Emily Tennyson was no doll's-house wife. But Tennyson still lent his authority to the idealisation of Woman, and this stood in the way of a full and natural life for women far more subtly and formidably than the simple 'woman's-place-is-in-the-home' dogmatist. The insistence on reverence for womanhood, with its purity (something that it was expected to have though everyone agreed it was too much to expect of men), erected one vast falsehood somewhere at the centre of life. Woman could be passionate but not sexual: she must endure her husband's animal nature, loving him in spite of it. He in the meantime must hate it in himself and try to crush it 'as a vice of blood'. This, as far as one can make it out, was the Victorian attitude, and all the weight of Tennyson's moral teaching was thrown in to strengthen it. Hence the intolerable speech-making of King Arthur to his fallen Queen: intolerably pompous now, that is, though often found deeply moving then.

Arthur is intolerable because he is obviously hopeless at personal relationships. He is heavy and dull, without spice. Tennyson was not like this himself but he often wrote as though he were. The bardic authority weighed on him like an archbishop's robes, and made it as difficult to be natural. Or rather, worse, it made the heavy pontifical tone become second nature. One wonders what Gladstone really thought when in the midst of his troubles with the Franchise Bill of 1884 he received eight lines of rhyme from the Laureate, starting:

> Steersman, be not precipitate in thine act.

He wrote back to say that he thought it a great honour. Times, statesmen and poets change. One would like to have a reply from Attlee to similar advice from T. S. Eliot. Of course, what makes the heaviness of touch so ludicrous is that the verse itself is so very undistinguished. It is like the lines to F. D. Maurice, written at a time when Maurice was a victim of Victorian religious persecution:

> Come, when no graver cares employ,
> Godfather, come and see your boy;
>   Your presence will be sun in winter,
> Making the little one leap for joy.

The heart is in the right place, but the verse is doggerel. The bardic position was simply an impossible one. When T. S. Eliot wrote badly the critic would say 'Poor Tom's a-cold'; and, even with the aura of 'significance' that surrounded Eliot, the comparison was not exactly a ludicrous one. In the case of Tennyson, however, the bardic role was that degree grander, larger-than-life. To sustain it he must write well, and he so often did not.

But even this rightly-placed heart was often misled by the intellect. The patriotic heart would swell and throb when the brain told it that Britons must guard their own and take a strong line against France or Russia. But it was not half aware of the limitations of what 'their own' meant. In his youth, Tennyson had been enthusiastic for reform, but unsympathetic to the agitation which was the people's only means of frightening their wretched government into doing something for them. In *Maud* he wrote some lines about the condition of the poor in the industrial towns (Part I, *i*, 9):

> When the poor are hovell'd and hustled together, each sex like swine.

But he knew too little about it at first hand to be deeply and effectively moved. The passages in *Maud* reflect the temporary influence of Charles Kingsley upon him. When J. A. Froude, the Victorian historian, said that he and his generation found in Tennyson the voice of their deepest feeling, he was forgetting that 'his generation' included a majority of uneducated people whose 'deepest feelings' principally involved the need to keep alive and who would have made nothing out of Tennyson's literary tongue even if they had been able to read. Dickens and Kingsley did something to fight their battles. To Tennyson the relevant battles were grand affairs in the Crimea or the ones that never happened against the corrupt French nearer home. Tennyson, like Froude, was quite out of touch with the majority of humble ordinary people.

For the war-mongering, which I think on balance *Maud* is guilty of, Tennyson has some excuse. Enthusiasm for the Crimean venture was at first very general, and appalling things were thought and said in this otherwise peaceful mid-century. Quoted in Asa Briggs' *Victorian People* is a sentence by Robert Pemberton Milnes [1854]: 'War goes on famously and I would have it go on—wars are serviceable, as thunderstorms are—there would be no breathing at Crewe Hall between Manchester and the Potteries, but for them'. But how it would have increased one's respect for Tennyson if, instead of encouraging the barbarism (he did it even in his nursery—reporting happily how the children were massacring Russians on the play-room floor), he had responded with heart and brain to the reports of dreadful sufferings in the military hospitals which were being published bravely and persistently in *The Times*. But no: all that came from him was a glorification of the blind heroism made possible by brainless military discipline:

> Theirs not to make reply,
> Theirs not to reason why,
> Theirs but to do and die.
> Into the valley of Death
> Rode the six hundred.

With all this, along with the reaction against most things Victorian, it is not surprising that later generations 'came out' against Tennyson. As we have seen, criticism was rarely silent during his own lifetime. Even when he had become most securely a national institution, there were Samuel Butler and his friends deciding that it wouldn't do to like Blake because of a connection at three removes with Tennyson. There were others like Edward Fitzgerald who thought that Tennyson had been in decline since 1842. But generally, acceptance and national pride grew, and at his death preachers all over the country were praising a great Christian, a great Englishman, and a great 'singer' (in that order). It is natural that when the reaction came it should have been extreme.

The reaction was partly an assertion of humour in the face of solemnity. Max Beerbohm's *Mr. Tennyson reading 'In Memoriam' to his Sovereign* (facing p. 81) set the tone: it has the stifled ecstasy of laughter in church, and implies the sophisticated smartness which helps the bright young things of the present to make confident fun of their elders. Samuel Butler's irreverence found an echo in Shaw's: any healthy mind, he said, is more interested in *Tit Bits* than in *Idylls of the King*. There was also a sense that Tennyson belonged to things gone dead, and one *wanted* to laugh at him or debunk him. 'To care for his poetry is to be old-fashioned, and to belittle him is to be in the movement', wrote A. C. Bradley in 1914 (in *The Reaction against Tennyson*; a lecture to the English Association). In the Apology of 1922, Hardy quotes two lines from *In Memoriam* and adds in brackets 'if one may quote Tennyson in this century'. In Hardy's poem, *An Ancient to Ancients*, a Victorian speaks to his contemporaries:

The bower we shrined to Tennyson,
   Gentlemen,
Is roof-wrecked; damps there drip upon
Sagged seats, the creeper-nails are rust;
The spider is sole denizen.

Since then, F. R. Leavis has done much by serious critical argument and demonstration to ensure that a further generation should see Tennyson as a writer outside the main and valuable stream in English poetry. He has been 'placed' as a major talent (though not a major poet), weakened by a whole complex of forces, psychological, literary and social. W. H. Auden, introducing a selection of Tennyson's poems in 1946, gave this as his assessment: 'He had the finest ear of any English Poet; he was also undoubtedly the stupidest; there was little about melancholia that he didn't know; there was little else that he did'.

All the same, Tennyson abides. We still find him memorable. We can still say 'Tennysonian' and mean something distinctive by it. So many phrases, from 'kind hearts and coronets' to 'a waste land' and 'a handful of dust', have become part of our mid-twentieth-century language. We still find ourselves impressed by the sheer number of memorable poems he wrote. Turning over the pages of a Complete Tennyson is like going again to some nineteenth-century opera one has half-forgotten: there is this famous air and that celebrated chorus, and the tunes follow one another in astonishing supply.

When we look at the other face of the Janus we see in fact much to admire and value. For instance, the hard-headed common-sense, with a touch of humour to give it a cutting edge. It is not what one first thinks of in connection with Tennyson but it is there, not only in the two *Northern Farmer* poems, superbly pointed, vivid poems both, without a false note in them, but in that surprising poem *St. Simeon Stylites*. St. Simeon's feat of enduring.

   Rain, wind, frost, heat, hail, damp, and sleet, and snow

on top of a pillar forty cubits high is the *reductio ad absurdum* of

the monastic ideal. Like the tempter in *Murder in the Cathedral*
he urges a martyrdom of mortification in order to ensure
his passage to heaven. The ulcers have eaten through his
skin and the brethren have marvelled greatly. And Fitzgerald
tells us 'A.T. read it laughing'. In spirit, the poem is close to
burlesque, though it is subtly done, and only the extravagances
of the:

> Coughs, aches, stitches, ulcerous throes and cramps

make it easy to catch the note of laughter in the poet's (though
not the speaker's) voice.

St. Simeon Stylites, written about 1833, was one of the earliest
dramatic monologues, an exploratory poem in the form which
Browning was later to make his own. As an experimental
versifier, Tennyson incurred fierce criticism in his own time, yet
he has come to be thought of as an ultra-conservative who halted
the development of English poetry for half-a-century. In a
purely technical sense, this is obviously untrue. He tried and
mastered a great many forms, and to the end of his life would
take up (triumphantly in *Boadicea*, for example) forms that were
both new and difficult. The *In Memoriam* verse-form, marvellously sustained over so long a poem, was his invention (even
though, unknown to him, it had been invented before). The odd
patchwork method of *Maud*, so effective and right in conveying
the spontaneity of a moody, unstable mind, was also a boldness
which met with the same snarls of annoyance from baffled readers
as twentieth-century poetry habitually does today.

It is interesting, too, that, while criticism of Tennyson in this
century has argued that he is limited and regrettable because so
often 'escapist' and 'literary', he was in mid-nineteenth century
thought of as a modernist and one who specifically brought
modern life into poetry. Kingsley writing on Tennyson in 1850
might almost be any contemporary admirer writing on Eliot in
1930: 'He dares, in every page, to make use of modern words
and notions, from which the mingled clumsiness and archaism
of his compeers shrinks, as unpoetical'. Kingsley was to some

extent re-making the poet in his own image: at least he was giving emphasis to an occasional, rather than a permanent, characteristic. He uses 'poetical' language—but he was also a poet receptive and unconventional enough to make 'literary' poetry out of the new features of industrial England:

> Let the great world spin for ever down the ringing grooves of change.

I suppose with these lines from *Locksley Hall* Tennyson can claim to have made the first 'railway image' in English poetry: he tells how he first thought of the line on a dark night in 1830 waiting for the first train from Liverpool to Manchester.

But where Tennyson was most sensitive to new currents of thought was over the implications of the biological and geological discoveries of the early half of the century. Reading Lyell's *Principles*, he was far quicker than his contemporaries to see where these investigations were leading. Man was being pulled into nature, made more inescapably a part of the brute creation. Less and less did it seem easy to believe that he was God's special creature; less and less could it be assumed that the species had a natural dignity and significance. This works through *In Memoriam*, giving it its own special character; for the poem is not simply a lament for a dead individual but also for a broken image. Man was one thing and is now another; was a proud, quite special creature, is now seen as a part of nature. Part of a nature, moreover, in which no moral law or purpose can be found; and it is this that feeds the underlying pessimism of *Maud*. A very revealing saying of his, reported by his son, is this: 'The lavish profusion too in the natural world appals me, from the growths of the tropical forest to the capacity of man to multiply, the torrent of babies'. If life is the special gift of a powerful, personally involved creator, how can it be so utterly common? This profusion can come as a disturbing realisation even to us a century later, who have been so long used to the idea. As we see films which show, say, the fantastic processes of birth in shoals under water, perhaps with most of the new life coming into being only to feed some other equally thronging but meaningless variety, the whole puzzle of creation presses in upon us. How *can* there be moral or spiritual purpose in such a universe? How can we see anything other than a blind biological drive? 'Birth, copulation and death', as Eliot has it. Tennyson was very troubled indeed. At the basis of all his sensibility seems to be a swimming uncertainty about the things that mattered most: God, immortality, the nature of Man and the nature of Nature, the permanence of civilisation (which really meant British civilisation), the character and future of the British people. In the face of uncertainties, he generally asserted faith. It is the tension between belief and doubt that makes the poet's sensibility something stronger than is suggested by the usual word 'melancholy'. 'There was little about melancholia that he didn't know; there was little else that he did', said Auden. The judgement is brisk and authoritative, faintly arrogant, more than faintly untrue.

The man, then, his sensibility and his preoccupations, are both interesting and moving to us; it is partly for this that he survives. His art also leads us into other kinds of pleasures and experiences, and it may be, after all, still more on account of these that we return to him. His feeling for words was not Shakespearean. Donne, Keats, Hopkins, even Hardy, are his superiors in using the language creatively, with the rich and complex life which poets can command. As many again, and perhaps more, could be added to the list. Sufficient distinction remains to him even so.

Most obviously and most famously, there is the skill in sound. Sometimes a sort of manufactured beauty, a self-conscious *tour de force*, Tennysonian onomatopaeia does often 'bring off' a descriptive passage with rare brilliance:

> Dry clash'd his harness in the icy caves
> And barren chasms, and all to left and right
> The bare black cliff clang'd round him, as he based
> His feet on juts of slippery crag that rang
> Sharp-smitten with the dint of armed heels—
> And on a sudden, lo! the level lake,
> And the long glories of the winter moon.

These lines from *Morte d'Arthur* are so famous that comment may be unnecessary. But one can hardly read them, for the however-many'th time, without recognising them afresh as a sort of classic and marvellously effective. Hard consonants are seconded by the percussive force of monosyllables and the forward drive of run-on lines, to make real the harsh, jagged landscape and the effort of body and spirit. In the last two lines as the view changes to kindly horizontals of sky and lake, so the consonants become gentle, the vowel sounds lengthen, and the movement ceases to press. It is not just a technical and external virtuoso display, for the lake brings home and rest, and Tennyson has finely orchestrated his verse to make, like his own lotos-eaters:

> Music that kindlier on the spirit lies,
> Than tired eyelids upon tired eyes.

He can write more creatively than this, for this still registers as essentially as applied skill.

> About a stone-cast from the wall
>   A sluice with blacken'd waters slept,
> And o'er it many, round and small,
>   The cluster'd marish mosses crept.

In this passage from *Mariana*, as Robin Mayhead points out (in the *Pelican Guide to English Literature, Vol. 6*), the interaction of sound and sense is altogether subtler: 'the clustering of consonants, and the heavy, clogged movement imposed on the reader who tries to articulate the words clearly aloud, play a large part in creating the total impression of thick stagnation'. But this remains most vividly Tennyson's territory:

>   a glimmering land,
> Lit with a low large moon . . .
> The ragged rims of thunder brooding low,
>   With shadow-streaks of rain . . .
>   realms of upland, prodigal in oil,
> And hoary to the wind.

PALACE OF ART

His seascapes too carry a feeling and strength of imagination which go beyond mere scene painting. The sea counted for much in Tennyson's imagination. From *Crossing the Bar* with its:

> Such a tide as moving seems asleep

—we can trace the sea as a dominant image in his mind, back to the earliest poems of all:

> The mighty waste of moaning waters lay
> So goldenly in moonlight, whose clear lamp
> With its long line of vibratory lustre
> Trembled on the dun surface, that my spirit
> Was buoyant with rejoicings.

THE DEVIL AND THE LADY

Such lines carry a world of feeling. They do paint a vivid scene, but more essentially they work in the characteristic way of romantic poetry to carry one into the poet himself. His sense of beauty in the creation around him, and a yearning, desolate consciousness of isolation: this is the 'private' poet of these early years, and it remains the most commonly admired and appreciated part of Tennyson's work. No wonder, for it would be strange if readers of poetry, however little given to like the Victorians, should not find some spell cast by such passages. At very least there is the magic of the story-book:

> Only reapers, reaping early
> In among the bearded barley,
> Hear a song that echoes cheerly
> From the river winding clearly,
>   Down to tower'd Camelot;
> And by the moon the reaper weary,
> Piling sheaves in uplands airy,
> Listening, whispers 'Tis the fairy
>   Lady of Shalott'.

At most there is a beauty of image and sound that is individual and perfect:

The woods decay, the woods decay and fall,
The vapours weep their burthen to the ground,
Man comes and tills the field and lies beneath,
And after many a summer dies the swan.

TITHONUS

'Tennyson knew his magician's business.' What we tend to overlook is that the magician's early 'private' poems are *about* something. Or rather, that the ones we remember as 'pure poetry' are an expression of ways of thought and feeling that were fundamental to the struggling development both of him and of his age. What we also tend to underestimate, is that the 'public' poems of later years are also poetic. Again, this needs qualification, for they do contain a great deal of ruminating, moralising and story-telling in verse, which is not the same thing. But there is still, at best, a fusion of thought and feeling that finds its expression in genuine poetry. Even the *Idylls* achieve some poetic glow from time to time. *Demeter and Other Poems* (1889), the last volume published during Tennyson's lifetime, is no arid rattling of dry bones, and it contains surely one of the finest of all. He decided to print an early poem called *The Progress of Spring* and dedicated it to his friend Mary Boyle, with a new poem. Reading this, with its warm feeling and easy, supple movement, one may well forget that the other face of the Janus is there still to be despised. Having paused long enough to admire, one may indeed wonder whether one does well to despise at all.

Bibliography

The basis of our knowledge of Tennyson's life is *Alfred, Lord Tennyson: A Memoir* (Hallam Tennyson), 2 vols. (Reprint House International, New York). Sir Charles Tennyson's *Alfred Tennyson* (Shoe String Press, Hamden, Conn.) draws freely on this, but adds a great deal of important new material. An entertaining modern book is Joanna Richardson's *The Pre-Eminent Victorian* (Lawrence Verry, Inc., Mystic, Conn., 1962).

For criticism, by far the most appreciative and profound study is Valerie Pitt's *Tennyson Laureate* (Univ. of Toronto, Canada, 1963). Hugh I'A Fausset's *Tennyson: A Modern Portrait* (Russell & Russell, New York) and J. H. Buckley's *Tennyson, The Growth of a Poet* (Harvard Univ. Press, Cambridge, Mass., 1960) are interesting and valuable. P. F. Baum's *Tennyson Sixty Years After* (Univ. of North Carolina Press, Chapel Hill, N.C., 1948) is hostile: its criticisms and arguments are usually worth attention. An invaluable collection of essays on Tennyson by his contemporaries is *Tennyson: The Critical Heritage*, ed. Prof. J. D. Jump (Barnes & Noble, 1967).

Among shorter studies is Dr. F. R. Leavis' criticism of Tennyson to be found in *New Bearings in English Poetry* (Univ. of Mich. Press, Ann Arbor, Mich.) and in an essay called 'Thought and Emotional Quality' (*Scrutiny* XIII, i). T. S. Eliot has an essay on 'In Memoriam' in *Essays Ancient and Modern*, reprinted in *Critical Essays of the Poetry of Tennyson*, ed. John Killham (Barnes & Noble, New York). Basil Willey's *More Nineteenth Century Studies* (Harper & Row, New York) has an excellent chapter on Tennyson.

More specialised works that are nevertheless strongly recommended are E. F. Shannon's *Tennyson and the Reviewers* (Shoe String Press, Hamden, Conn., 1952), and R. W. Rader's *Tennyson's Maud: The Biographical Genesis* (Univ. of California Press, Berkeley, Calif., 1963).

For background reading Asa Briggs' *Victorian People* (Harper & Row, New York), and G. M. Young's *Victorian England* (Oxford Univ. Press, New York) are both scholarly and lively. Basil Willey's book already mentioned and his *Nineteenth Century Studies* (Columbia Univ. Press, New York, 1949) go more deeply into the thought of the period. For a complete survey of the literature there is Volume 6 of *The Pelican Guide to English Literature: from Dickens to Hardy* (Penguin Books, Baltimore, Md., 1963). This contains a chapter on Tennyson by Robin Mayhead.

Index

GENERAL INDEX

Albert, Prince Consort, 87, 104, 110
Allen, Matthew, 63
Anti-Maud, 88
Apostles, The, 27–30, 32, 33, 64
Arnold, Matthew, 114, 133
Auden, W. H., 54, 64, 149, 152, 157
Austin, Alfred, 143

Baum, Paull F., 73, 74, 75, 138, 156
Beerbohm, Max, 148
Blackwood's Magazine, 65, 66
Blake, William, 128, 148
Boyle, Mary, 155
Bradley, A. C., 111, 113, 148, 156
Bridges, Dr. Robert, 143
Briggs, Asa, 147, 157
Brontë, Charlotte, 73, 75
Brontë, Emily, 11, 12
Brookfield, W. H., 27, 28, 30
Browning, Robert, 82, 134, 139, 150
Buckley, J. H., 48, 156
Buffon, G. L., 86
Butler, Samuel, 12, 83, 129, 148
Byron, Lord, 29, 60, 128

Cadogan, Lord, 106
Caine, Hall, 143
Cameron, Julia Margaret, 104
Carlyle, Thomas, 32, 59, 63, 70, 140
Christian Remembrancer, The, 87
Coleridge, Samuel Taylor, 128
Croker, John Wilson, 66

Dabbs, Dr. George, 142
Dante, 128
Darwin, Charles, 83, 86
Dickens, Charles, 128, 147
Donne, John, 152
Dryden, John, 114, 144

Edinburgh Review, 66, 68
Eliot, T. S., 38, 146, 150, 152, 156
Empson, William, 17

Ferdinand VII of Spain, 33
Fitzgerald, Edward, 26, 30, 32, 67, 73, 104, 148, 150
Forster, E. M., 21, 77
Forster, John, 102
Froude, J. A., 147

Gentleman's Magazine, 22
Gilbert and Sullivan, 67–8, 143
Gladstone, W. E., 30, 31, 32, 60, 111, 142, 146
Gray, Thomas, 75

Hallam, Arthur, 14, 27, 30–3, 61–2, 65, 71, 72, 79, 141
Hallam, Henry, 61, 63
Hardy, Thomas, 143, 148–9, 152
Hogg's Weekly Instructor, 66
Homer, 61
Hopkins, Gerard Manley, 38, 152
Horace, 12
Hunt, Holman, 126, 143
Huxley, Aldous, 43, 52
Huxley, Thomas, 109, 143

Irving, Henry, 137–8, 139, 143

Jonson, Ben, 18
Jowett, Benjamin, 16, 23, 103, 104

Keats, John, 18, 32, 43, 44, 128, 152
Kemble, Fanny, 30
Kemble, John, 27–8, 29, 30
Kingsley, Charles, 104, 111–12, 147, 150
Knowles, Sir James, 65, 86

Lamarck, J. B., 86
Lear, Edward, 104, 126, 144
Leavis, F. R., 149, 156
Lewes, G. H., 109
Lucas, F. L., 52, 110
Lushington, Edmund, 79
Lushington, Franklin, 105
Lushington, Henry, 27
Lyell, Sir Charles, 86, 151

Malory, Thomas, 114
Maurice, F. D., 29, 146
Mayhead, Robin, 153, 157
Merivale, Charles, 27, 60
Mill, J. S., 65
Milnes, Richard Monckton, 27, 28
Milnes, Robert Pemberton, 147
Milton, 18, 35, 61, 113, 139
Mitford, Mary, 73, 78, 79
Morris, William, 114

Nicolson, Sir Harold, 27–8, 30, 31, 104, 156
North, Christopher, 65

Paley, William, 29
Peel, Sir Robert, 63
Pitt, Valerie, 70, 71, 156
Pope, Alexander, 16
Puccini, 132
Punch, 143

Quarterly Review, 65, 66

Ritchie, Lady, 105
Rossetti, Dante Gabriel, 14
Ruskin, John, 126

Scott, Sir Walter, 16
Sellwood, Emily, 60, 62, 83, 88, 102, 104, 107, 126, 143
Shakespeare, 19, 64, 70, 138, 139, 142, 144, 152
Shannon, E. F., 66, 69, 157
Shaw, G. B., 148
Shelley, Percy Bysshe, 16–17, 18, 28, 29, 35, 128
Sibelius, J., 35
Simeon, Sir John, 104, 107
Spedding, James, 27, 28, 65

Spenser, 18, 113
Stevenson, Robert Louis, 126
Strachey, Lytton, 31
Swift, Jonathan, 136

Tennant, R. J., 62
Tennyson, Arthur, 11, 15, 61
Tennyson, Cecilia, 79
Tennyson, Charles (poet's brother), 14, 23, 26, 61, 62, 79
Tennyson, Charles (poet's uncle), 10
Tennyson, Sir Charles (poet's grandson and biographer), 12, 23, 25, 80, 86, 108, 128, 133, 156
Tennyson, Edward, 14, 61
Tennyson, Mrs. Elizabeth (poet's mother), 9, 11, 14
Tennyson, Emily, 14
Tennyson, Lady Emily (*see* Emily Sellwood)
Tennyson, Frederick, 11, 13, 14, 16, 23, 26, 61, 63, 73
Tennyson, George (poet's grandfather), 9, 10, 15, 61, 62
Tennyson, George Clayton the younger, 9, 10, 11, 13–14, 61
Tennyson, Hallam (poet's grandson and biographer), 11, 23, 25, 28, 32, 64, 143, 156
Tennyson, Septimus, 14, 51
Thirlwall, Connop, 29
Thompson, W. H., 27, 28, 32
Thomson, James, 16
Times, The, 9, 10, 38, 106, 128, 142, 143, 147
Trench, Richard Chenevix, 27, 41, 42

Victoria, Queen, 72, 87, 104, 110, 142
Virgil, 128

Westminster Review, 68
Wilde, Oscar, 42, 49
Wollstonecraft, Mary, 68
Wordsworth, Charles, 60
Wordsworth, Christopher, 60
Wordsworth, William, 29, 34, 60, 88, 128, 143

Yeats, J. B., 140–1
Young, G. M., 82, 86, 157

Airy, fairy Lilian, 96, 144
Alton Locke, 111–12
Ancient Sage, 135
Armageddon, 24, 25, 33
Aylmer's Field, 129–32

Becket, 139
Boadicea, 150
Bridesmaid, The, 62
Britons, guard your own, 105

Charge of the Light Brigade, The, 106, 107
Crossing the Bar, 18, 141–3, 154
Cup, The, 138

Death of Oenone, The, 137
Demeter and other poems, 137, 155
Despair, 134
Devil and the Lady, The, 18–25, 154
Dora, 59
Dying Swan, The, 35

Enoch Arden, 132–3

Grandmother, The, 133

Hands all round, 105
Happy, 136
Harold, 139
Home, 26

Idylls of the King, 42, 110, 113–27, 129, 139, 142, 148, 155
In Memoriam, 9, 26, 28, 30, 51, 60, 61, 62, 71, 72–8, 88, 89, 110, 143, 148, 150, 151
Isabel, 9, 36

Kraken, The, 59

Lady Clara Vere de Vere, 59, 131
Lady of Shalott, The, 38–41, 48, 49, 50, 56, 59, 154
Land of Hope and Glory, 105
Leonine Elegiacs, 35
Lines on Cambridge of 1830, 27
Locksley Hall, 54–6, 59, 66, 129, 151
Locksley Hall Sixty Years After, 29, 56, 136–7, 141
Lotos-Eaters, The, 17, 42–6, 48, 49, 50, 56, 59

Mariana, 34, 35, 36–9, 51, 56, 59, 153
Mariana in the South, 59
Maud, 51, 56, 85, 88–102, 104, 109, 111–12, 129, 145, 147, 150, 151
May-Queen, The, 59, 144
Miller's Daughter, The, 59
Mine Host, 64
Morte d'Arthur, 59, 62, 114, 115, 117, 126, 153
My life is full of weary days, 35

Northern Farmer, 149
Nothing will die, 35
Now sleeps the crimson petal, 18

Ode on the Death of the Duke of Wellington, 107–9
Ode to Memory, 9, 59
Oenone, 57–8, 59
Oriana, 32
Outcast, The, 26
Owl, The, 65

Palace of Art, The, 40–4, 48, 49, 56, 153
Perdidi Diem, 24
Poems by Two Brothers, 22–3, 25
Princess, The, 66–71, 87, 145
Progress of Spring, The, 155

Queen Mary, 139, 140

Riflemen form!, 106

St. Simeon Stylites, 59, 149, 150
Sea Dreams, 133
Silent Voices, The, 143
Song (A Spirit haunts the year's last hours), 35
Supposed Confessions of a Second-rate Sensitive Mind, 49–50, 56, 59, 80, 86–7

Timbuctoo, 32, 60
Tithonus, 51–3, 56, 59, 154–5
Two Voices, The, 46–9, 50–1, 56, 59, 62, 135

Ulysses, 52–4, 56, 59, 62, 63

Vision of Sin, The, 59